Despite the fact that most b
on fishing emphasize anglin
artif... lures, the use
... se

fisherman's enjoyment of his favorite sport. Even the angler who never or rarely uses live bait, but depends upon artificial lures, will benefit from a knowledge of a fish's natural foods. Most lures are designed to resemble natural baits or imitate their action in the water. Therefore, the more the angler knows about the habits of natural baits, the more proficient will he be in locating the feeding grounds of fish and in imitating the live baits with his artificial lures. Fish, after all, gather where their food is plentiful and strike best at a lure that most closely resembles this food.

Natural Baits for Fishermen is, without question, one of the most valuable books ever made available to the angler—whether he is interested in salt or fresh water fishing, whether he prefers to use natural baits or lures. It is a complete and authoritative work covering fishing conditions in every part of the country in all seasons of the year.

NATURAL BAITS
FOR FISHERMEN

NATURAL BAITS FOR FISHERMEN

by

Vlad Evanoff

Illustrated by the author

A. S. BARNES and COMPANY
NEW YORK

Library of Congress Catalog Card Number: 59-12401

Printed in the United States of America

Foreword

MILLIONS OF FISHERMEN IN BOTH FRESH AND SALT WATER USE LIVE OR natural baits when they try their luck. Only a small minority of anglers never or rarely use such natural baits. Sooner or later every fisherman finds that he can catch more fish and have more fun if he uses natural baits on many of his fishing trips.

But when he tries to find out which baits are best, where they can be obtained, how they are kept or preserved, and how they are used, he runs into difficulties. Such information is either obtained the hard way through trial and error or bit by bit from scattered books, magazines and other printed sources. Hundreds of books have been written on using artificial lures. But very rarely has a book such as this been devoted entirely to natural baits.

There is a common belief among fishermen who use artificial lures that using natural baits is too easy and requires little skill or study. But those anglers who have used natural baits for a long time soon discover that there are many things to learn about such baits. The use of natural baits often requires as much skill and knowledge as the use of artificial lures. Those anglers who have made a study of fresh and salt water baits usually catch more and bigger fish than their fellow anglers.

There is a tendency to get into a rut when using natural baits. Most anglers stick to a few natural baits and rarely try other kinds. But the most successful fishermen in both fresh and salt water know how to use a wide variety of natural baits.

The author hopes that this guide to the fresh and salt water natural baits will provide the necessary information for using these baits.

VLAD EVANOFF

Acknowledgments

The author wishes to express his appreciation to the state fish and game and conservation departments which supplied information and material which proved extremely helpful in writing this book. The bulletins of the California Fish and Game Department were especially helpful.

Thanks are also due to the U. S. Fish and Wildlife Service which provided valuable information and material aiding the writer immeasurably.

Also to the editors of *Sports Afield* magazine for permission to use some of the illustrations which appeared in their *Sports Afield Fishing Annual*.

Contents

List of Illustrations

Part One—Natural Fresh Water Fishing Baits

PART ONE

NATURAL
Fresh Water
FISHING BAITS

Chapter I

EARTHWORMS

BY FAR THE MOST POPULAR NATURAL BAIT USED IN FRESH-WATER FISHing is the earthworm. It is one of the best all-around baits that an angler can use. Most of the other live baits are limited to certain species of fish, but worms are taken by almost every fresh-water fish. Add to this the fact that earthworms are found in most sections of the country, are usually easy to obtain, can be kept indefinitely, and you have the main reasons for their popularity.

The strange thing is that although worms are not commonly found in streams, lakes or rivers, most fish will take them without hesitation if they are properly presented. Yet almost the only time earthworms find their way into streams and lakes is during heavy rains when they are washed into such waters, although a few may crawl into the water by mistake or fall in when the overhanging sod banks along the water's edge break off and roll into the stream or lake.

However, whether or not the earthworm is found naturally in the water doesn't concern the average angler too much. All he knows is that earthworms are eagerly taken by most fresh-water fish and if he uses them he can have some fine sport and bring home fish. But it is important to know some of the more important details about earthworms—their habits, how they are found, kept and used on the hook.

CHARACTERISTICS AND HABITS

Earthworms live in many kinds of soils, but they generally prefer a rich, loamy clay soil which contains plenty of organic matter. They swallow this earth and extract the plant and animal matter from it for nourishment while the rest of the soil passes through and is expelled in the form of "castings." You can notice these small droppings around the burrow holes in almost any garden or lawn. Earthworms are usually scarce or absent in sandy soils.

Earthworms do not like extreme heat, cold or dry soil. Under any of these conditions you will usually find them deep in the ground. When the ground is wet they can be found near the surface. The best time to dig worms is early in the spring or during the fall months when there is plenty of rain. During the hot summer months when the ground is dry the worms go down deep, and this is the time of year when anglers have trouble getting them.

SPECIES

There are more than 2,000 varieties of earthworms found throughout the world and most of them are taken by fish. But some species are scarce, while others are too small to make practical baits. And the giant earthworm found in Australia is even too big, for it may reach 10 feet in length and have a diameter of one inch. In this country three kinds of worms are commonly found and used for bait.

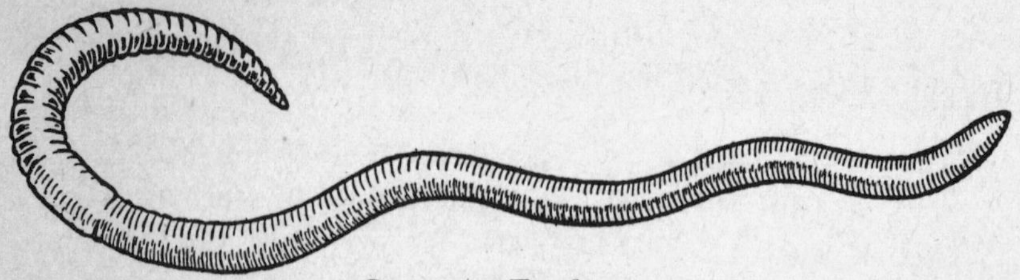

Common Earthworm

The one usually found in bait cans is the common earthworm (*Helodrilus caliginosus*) also known as the gardenworm, angleworm, garden hackle and fishworm. It is found in moist, fertile soil such as in gardens, fields and woodlands and is widely distributed throughout the United States. It may reach 5 or 6 inches in length, but most of those found will average 3 or 4 inches. Its color varies, being pink, gray, yellowish or blue, depending on where it is found. There are many other closely related species which can also be used as bait.

Probably next in popularity because of its size, distribution and availability is the night crawler (*Lumbricus terrestris*) also known as the nightwalker, rainworm and dew-worm. It is numerous in some locations but may be scarce or absent in others. The night crawler may reach 10 inches in length, but most of those found average about 6 or 7 inches. Its color is pink near the tail blending into a dark red and

Night Crawler

purple near the head. The tip of the tail usually flattens out when it is first caught.

The other worm used for bait is the manure worm (*Eisenia foetida*) also called the fecal earthworm, stinkworm and dung worm. This worm is widely distributed but is not too common because it is found mostly in manure, stables, barnyards and sewage. This preference gives it a disagreeable odor, and the worm exudes an unpleasant yellow liquid when handled or cut. It is a thin, small worm and reaches only about 4 or 5 inches in length. It can easily be recognized by its dark bands separated by lighter rings. It is also somewhat softer than the other worms, but it is very lively and makes a good bait.

Manure Worm

Of course, the above aren't the only worms used for bait. There are many other species which make good bait, and practically any large earthworm dug from the soil can be used.

OBTAINING, KEEPING, PRESERVING

The most common method of obtaining worms for fishing is by good old-fashioned digging. This can be a simple job or a discouraging task depending on the location, type of soil and season of the year. The common earthworm is the type usually obtained by digging and it is often found in gardens which have a rich soil. Use a garden fork instead of a shovel. The fork will not cut as many worms as a shovel will.

Although worms have the power of regeneration and can grow a new tail and often even a new head, a large percentage of cut worms will die and can contaminate the healthy ones, so it is best to throw them away.

During the hot summer months when the worms are deep, you can often find them in the sod in low, damp spots around springs, ponds or other bodies of water. Or you can get a garden hose and soak the ground with water; then dig for worms a few hours later.

There are other methods of obtaining worms, such as driving a stake into the ground and rubbing the top of it with a board to produce vibrations which drive the worms out of the ground. There are also electrical devices on the market which drive the worms out of the ground when rods are pushed into the earth and the current is turned on. Then there are various chemical solutions which are poured over the ground and which seep down into the burrows to chase worms to the surface. You can make your own solution by dissolving one bichloride of mercury tablet in a gallon of water. Strong solutions of mustard and water also bring worms to the surface when poured into their burrows. After using these solutions the worms should be washed immediately to remove the irritating substances. The trouble with most of these methods, however, is that they do not always work and when they do, the worms are usually numerous and near the surface anyway. So it is just as simple and often quicker to dig them up.

The big night crawlers are not as easy to dig since they stay down deep during the daytime. But at night, especially in the spring of the year during heavy rains, they come out of their burrows to mate and migrate. The warm, moist, quiet nights when the ground is damp bring them up in the greatest numbers. During the summer months when the ground is dry only a few will emerge from their burrows. But if there is a heavy shower or rain which soaks the ground they will reappear in large numbers.

The best places to look for night crawlers are golf links, gardens, lawns, parks or other spots where the grass is short and they are easy to spot. Walk softly as they are sensitive to vibrations and you will be able to get close enough to grab them. They are also sensitive to strong light and if you use a flashlight, shine the beam to one side and not directly at the worm. A weak light or a red light doesn't alarm them as much as a bright, white light.

Most of the night crawlers will be stretched out with their tail sections anchored inside their burrows. Grab them near the tail end close to the burrow and hold the worm taut for a few seconds until its muscles relax and it can be pulled out easily.

The manure worm can be found in old manure, stables, barnyards and sewage. This worm is often obtainable during the winter or early spring when the ground is frozen and other worms cannot be found. Because it lives in manure which holds moisture well, it is also available during the hot summer months when the ground is dry and other worms are down deep.

If you run out of worms on the fishing grounds, or do not have any and would like to try some as bait, you can often find a few by looking under old stumps, overturning flat rocks, boards, or decayed plants and leaves. The damp soil along the banks of streams and lakes often contains worms which can be dug with a board or stick. You can also try pulling up weeds or clumps of grass and searching in the roots for worms.

Of course, many anglers prefer to buy their worms from bait dealers or tackle shops, but if you do a lot of fishing it is cheaper to raise your own worms either outdoors or indoors. The simplest method, which entails little work or time if your ground already contains worms, is to pick a spot where you know they are present and place some wide, flat boards over it. Then empty your dishwater over this spot until the soil is well saturated. The worms will come to the top and all you have to do is lift the boards and pick them up. Ordinary water will also do the trick if the worms are numerous, but dishwater contains nourishment which will attract worms in the immediate vicinity. The water should be poured for several days in succession for best results.

However, the best method for a dependable supply of worms is to construct a worm box and sink it in the ground. Such a wooden box can easily be made using hardwoods, which will last longest in the ground. You can also coat the outside of the box with tar or wax to help preserve it. A good-sized box which will handle plenty of worms would be about 4 feet long, 3 feet wide and 3 feet deep. It can be smaller or larger depending on how many worms you want to keep. When building the box make sure that there are no cracks through which the worms can escape. A couple of holes should be bored in the bottom of the box for drainage and these should be covered with copper-wire screening.

Now bury the box in a shady, well-drained spot leaving only a few inches of the top of the box extending above the ground. Then fill the box with alternate layers of sod and soil. Layers of decayed leaves can

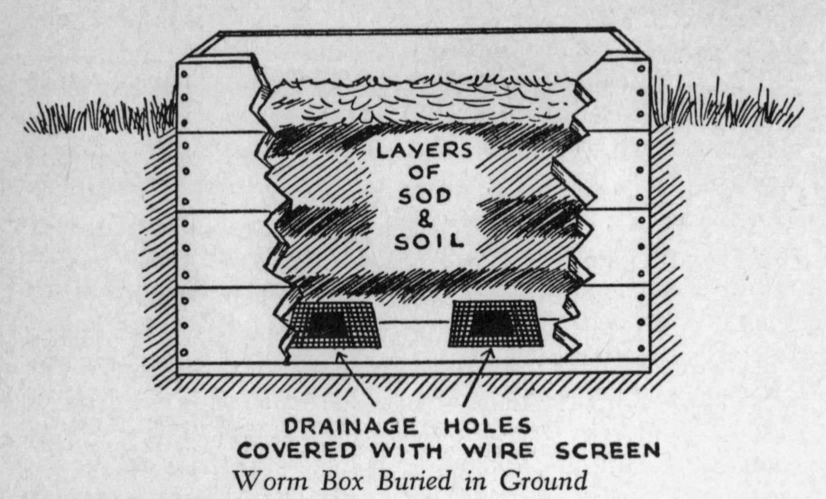

Worm Box Buried in Ground

be used instead of the sod. You can use plain moss in the box instead of sod and soil, but then you will have to feed the worms more often.

Finally, put a few hundred worms in the box and let them burrow into the soil. A damp burlap bag or a layer of leaves can be used to cover the soil and keep it moist. During the dry, hot summer months you may have to add some water, while during the rainy seasons you can cover the box to prevent it from flooding. If you leave the box outdoors during the winter, cover it with a thick layer of manure or leaves to keep out the frost.

Worms can also be kept indoors in wooden boxes, galvanized wash tubs, metal drums cut lengthwise or similar containers. These can be painted inside and outside to prevent them from rusting. The containers can be filled with soil and some decayed leaves, rotted straw or a small amount of manure. The worms need not be fed if they are being kept for short periods of time, but if kept for a long time you can feed them vegetable shortening or lard mixed with cornmeal. Bread crumbs, chicken mash and ground oats can also be used. This box can be kept in the cellar, garage, barn or any other place where it is cool. You should add some water from time to time to keep the soil moist.

The above methods are most suited to the person who does considerable fishing or has to provide bait for several persons. If you just need worms for a few fishing trips you can dig or buy several hundred and keep them in much smaller containers for a few months. Just place them in the containers with the soil and feed them and sprinkle some water on the soil occasionally. A few hours spent digging in the spring of the year when worms are numerous will generally provide enough bait for the rest of the fishing season.

When you first remove earthworms from the soil you will notice that they are filled with earth which they have swallowed when feeding and burrowing. They make fair bait fresh from the soil, but they become more attractive, livelier and tougher if they are "scoured" before using. To do this get an earthenware crock or flowerpot and obtain some sphagnum moss from a florist or nursery. Wash the moss and wring out the excess water. Now place the moss in the crock or flowerpot. Then put in the worms you intend to use on a fishing trip. After three or four days in the moss the worms will get rid of the earth inside them and become almost transparent, as well as tough and lively. If you must keep the worms in the moss longer than three or four days, feed them some milk.

The ordinary tin can is still one of the most popular containers used to transport worms to the fishing grounds. It is suitable if you are still-fishing from the bank or a rowboat. But a trout fisherman who wades in the water and must have his hands free for fishing, needs something less bulky. A flat, tobacco can with holes punched in the cover is handy, since it takes up little room and can be carried in a pocket. There are on the market many kinds of small bait boxes for worms. One of the most popular is the type which is held by the angler's belt

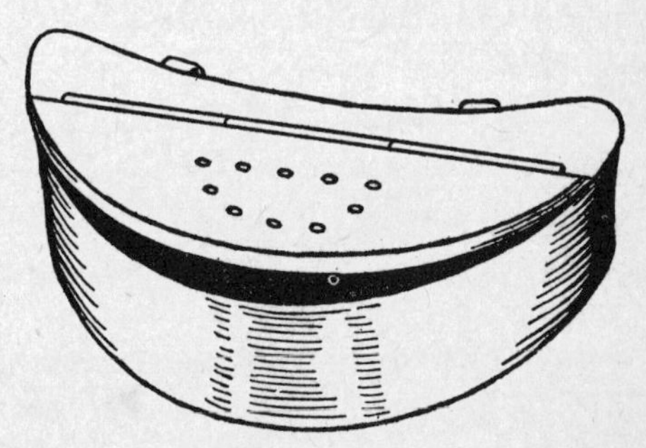

Belt-Type Bait Box

and is curved to fit the contour of his body. It is usually made from metal or plastic and has a perforated lid on a hinge. Any of these containers can be filled partly with earth if the worms are freshly dug or with moss or grass if they have been scoured. It is important to keep the containers out of the sun as much as possible to help prevent the heat from killing the worms.

METHODS OF HOOKING

Every angler has his own pet methods of hooking worms for the fish he is seeking. For trout fishing the worms should generally be hooked lightly under the light-colored sexual collar. The point and barb should be allowed to protrude. This method usually works best in streams where the worm is allowed to float naturally with the current. Sometimes when the trout are fussy, especially in quiet waters where they can pick up the bait at their leisure, the point and barb can be covered.

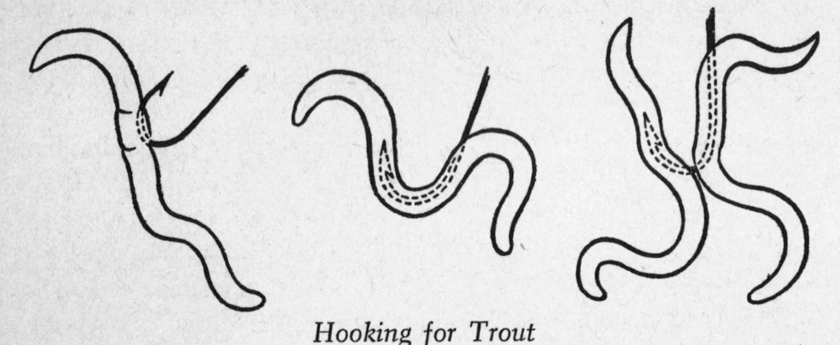

Hooking for Trout

Not because the fish can see the point and hook but because they may feel the point and spit the bait out: The point and barb can also be buried in the head of the worm when you want a bait that will not snag the weeds or other obstructions.

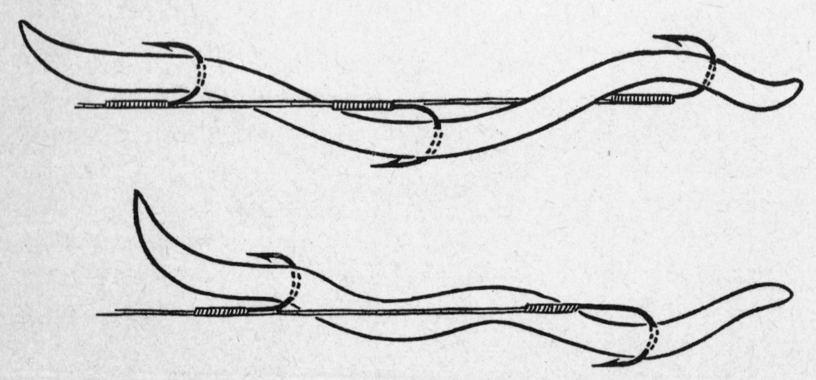

Hooking on Double and Gang Hooks

Generally one worm on a hook is best for trout, but there are times when two worms on a single hook produce better results. The smaller earthworms, between 2 and 4 inches, are best for trout, but night crawlers can be used for large trout. A gang hook with two or three single hooks attached to the same snell or leader is best for hooking these larger worms. It is also useful when trout strike short, just nipping off the tail of the worm. A gang hook also holds the worm better when casting any distance, since the worm hooked in three places has less chance of being snapped off. Check your state fish and game laws when using more than one hook to see if it is legal on the waters you intend to fish.

For black bass, 2 or 3 night crawlers placed on a hook so that the ends are free and allowed to wiggle are highly effective. When using the smaller varieties of worms even more can be put on a hook.

Hooking for Bass, Bullheads and Catfish

Large hooks in sizes 1 and 1/0 are best when using worms in such numbers. A single night crawler can also be hooked under the collar as for trout and cast out lightly, then allowed to drift with the current or worked back slowly toward the angler in quiet waters. Bass and pickerel will sometimes hit a worm worked in this manner.

Worms are also used for bass, trout, pickerel, pike and walleyes in combination with a spinner. Several worms draped over a large hook behind a June bug spinner, and trolled slowly over likely-looking spots, produce fish on many occasions.

For pan fish, like sunfish, yellow perch and rock bass, small whole worms or half-sections of larger ones are generally best. They will take night crawlers, but their mouths are too small to swallow the bait and they usually just nip off the ends. Even the smaller worms are readily stolen off the hook by the pan fish. The best method for such bait thieves is to loop the worm on the hook along the shank, allowing only short sections of the head and tail to wiggle.

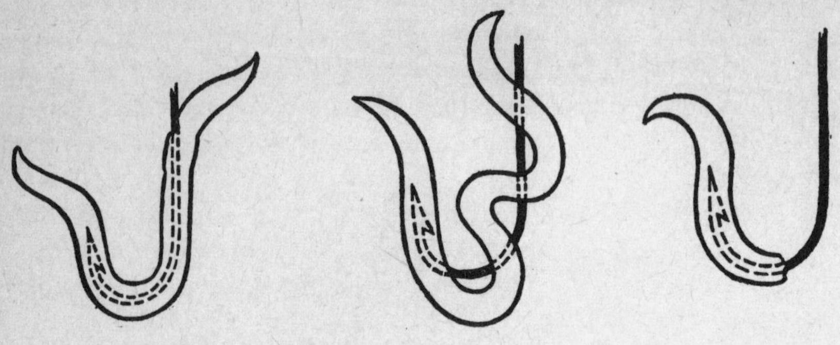

Hooking for Panfish

For bullheads and catfish, several worms on a hook work best. These fish have big mouths and can swallow hooks baited with plenty of worms.

When using worms for most fish, the livelier the worms the more strikes you will get. So the best method of hooking is the one which keeps the worm alive the longest possible time and still hooks a striking fish. Worms that have died or wiggle feebly should be removed from the hook and replaced with fresh ones. Sometimes you can make the fish strike a dead or feeble worm by moving the bait up and down or from side to side to attract attention, but you can't beat fresh, lively worms on a hook if you want to catch plenty of fish.

Chapter II

MINNOWS

Next to earthworms in popularity as bait are the minnows. Indeed, if they weren't somewhat harder to obtain and keep, or more expensive to buy than worms, minnows would probably be used more than any other bait. Most game fish feed on minnows to a great extent and practically all the other fresh-water fish eat them when they can get them. This is especially true of the larger fish which require plenty of food. Another factor which makes the minnow such a good bait is that when it is impaled on a hook it usually swims around energetically, attracting fish from a distance. And finally, minnows are found in most lakes, rivers and streams throughout the country.

CHARACTERISTICS AND HABITS

Most anglers call any small fish a few inches long a minnow. But a true minnow belongs to the family *Cyprinidae* which includes the carps and goldfish, as well as other large fish like the squawfish and white salmon, which may reach 4 or 5 feet in length and weigh up to 80 pounds. And if you go by size alone you will be including the young of game fish in your bait pail, which is something no sportsman wants to do.

Every angler who uses minnows should become familiar with the characteristics and structure of these forage fishes. Minnows have one dorsal fin, usually in the middle of the back, and it has less than 10 soft rays. The carp and goldfish are exceptions, having dorsal fins with more than 10 rays and single spines in the dorsal and anal fins. Also minnows have no teeth in the jaws and no scales on the head.

Minnows are found in all kinds of water from quiet ponds to the swiftest streams. Some species prefer the lakes, others are found in the larger rivers, while still others frequent the streams or brooks. When it comes to food, they'll eat land and water insects, small fish, fish eggs, snails, algae, small crustaceans, plankton, plants and even mud, sand or other debris from which they obtain organic matter.

SPECIES

There are over 1,000 species of minnows throughout the world with more than 300 found in North and Central America. Although most of them can be used for bait, some are more numerous and better suited for this purpose than others. The best bait minnows are those which are silvery or light in color, active and hardy on the hook and can stand handling, crowding and other unfavorable conditions. The following list includes the most popular and common minnows used for bait.

NORTHERN CREEK CHUB

(Semotilus atromaculatus atromaculatus)

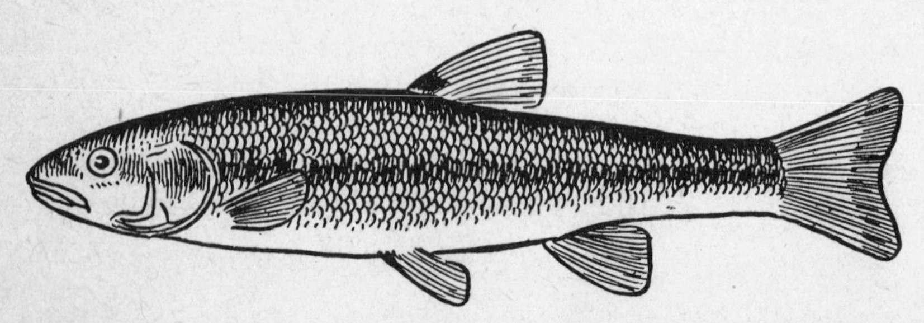

This minnow is often called the horned dace, common chub, horned chub or just plain chub. It can be recognized by its large mouth which extends back to the eye, the black spot at the base of the dorsal fin and the barbel just above the corners of the mouth. It has an olive-green back, steel-blue sides and a white belly. The creek chub is a large minnow, the females reaching 5 inches and the males 11 inches in length. It is found in creeks and rivers throughout the north, south, and central parts of the country. It is a hardy, lively minnow which is widely used for bait and can be easily caught on hook and line.

NORTHERN PEARL DACE

(Margariscus margarita nachtriebi)

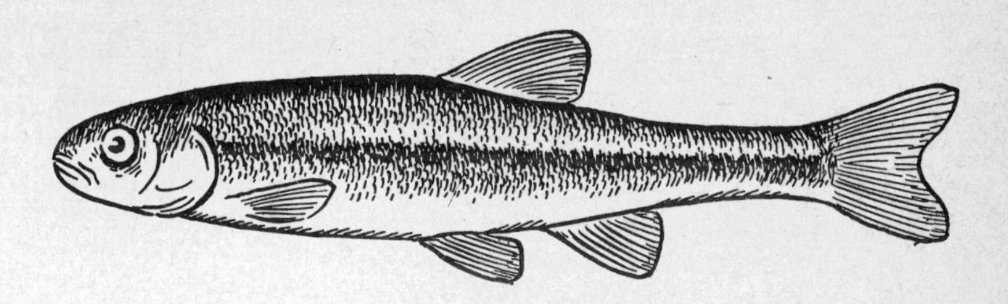

This minnow is also called leather back. It has a heavy body, a blunt snout and its color is a dusky silver mottled by darker scales. It is found in most of Canada east of the Rocky Mountains and in many of our northern states. The pearl dace prefers cool lakes, bogs and creeks. It is a hardy bait minnow.

THE HORNYHEAD CHUB

(Nocomis biguttatus)

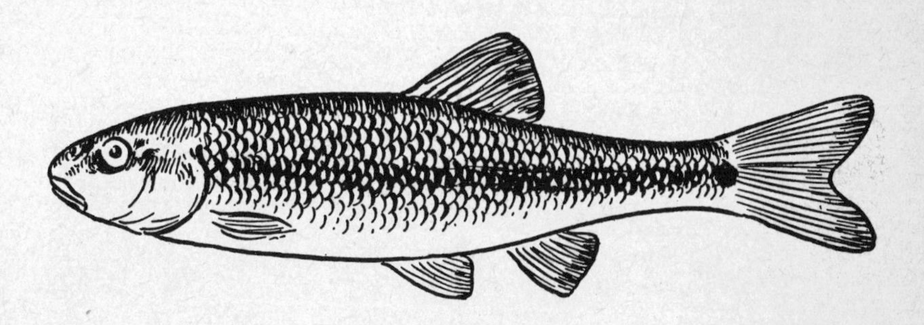

Also known as the jerker, this is a heavy-bodied minnow with a large head and big, distinct scales. It has barbels at the corners of the mouth and the color on the body is generally olivaceous. The young have a red tail and fin and there is a distinct round blackish spot at the base of the tail. This chub prefers the larger creeks and smaller rivers with gravel bottoms. It reaches a length of 8 or 10 inches and is a hardy bait minnow which stands up well on the hook or in a bait pail. It is found from the Rocky Mountains east to the Hudson River.

RIVER CHUB

(Nocomis micropogon)

This minnow resembles the hornyhead chub and is closely related to it. It also has a heavy body, blunt nose and large, distinct scales. But the spot at the base of its tail is not as clear or round as in the hornyhead chub. The river chub prefers the larger rivers, where it may reach 10 inches in length. It is a good bait minnow and can be readily caught on hook and line. It is found in many of our states from the Rocky Mountains east to New England and south to Virginia and Alabama.

SILVER CHUB

(Hybopsis storerianus)

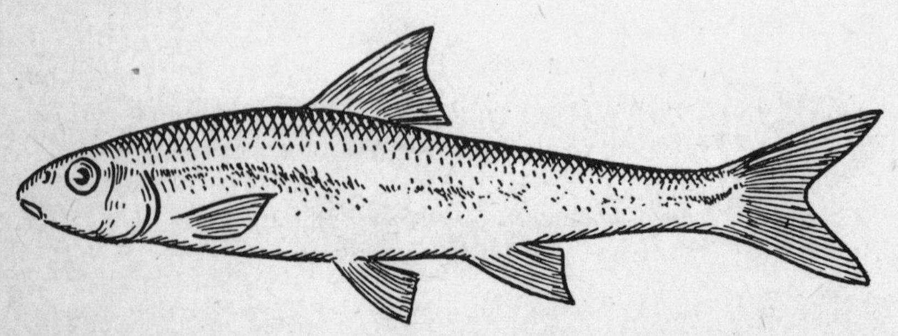

This minnow is also known as the storer's chub and is a silvery, attractive bait fish which may reach 8 or 10 inches in length. It is a slim minnow, with a short broad back that is greenish in color. It lives well in captivity and is active on a hook. It is found from the Red River drainage in Canada to the southern shore of Lake Ontario and southward to Alabama, Oklahoma and Wyoming.

WESTERN BLACKNOSE DACE

(Rhinichthys atratulus meleagris)

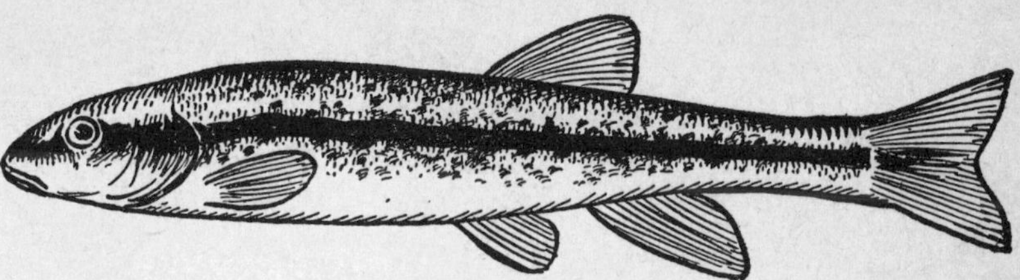

Also known as the striped dace, the blacknose dace is a fairly small minnow rarely reaching more than 3 inches in length. It is a slim minnow with a dusky back, black spots all over and a dark streak on the side of the body from the snout to the tail. This minnow prefers the cool, clear brooks and is often found in trout streams. It ranges from the Lake of the Woods region south to Nebraska and through most of the tributaries of the Great Lakes to the northern part of the Ohio River system. The eastern blacknose dace *(Rhinichthys atratulus atratulus)*, which resembles the western form, is found from Quebec southward, east of the Appalachian Divide, to Virginia.

NORTHERN REDBELLY DACE

(Chrosomus eos)

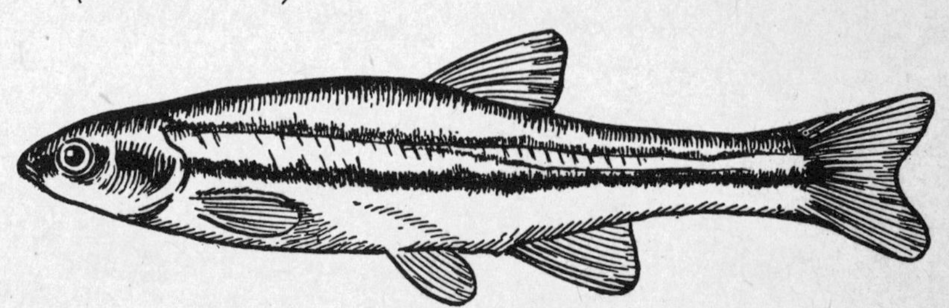

This minnow reaches 3 inches in length and is dark bronze in color with two distinct lateral bands running from head to tail. It is found in bog ponds and sluggish creeks in many parts of Canada and most of the northeastern and north-central states. A southern form, the southern redbelly dace *(Chrosomus erythrogaster)*, is found from Iowa to the southern parts of Wisconsin and Michigan to Pennsylvania and south to Alabama and Oklahoma.

WESTERN GOLDEN SHINER

(Notemigonus crysoleucas auratus)

This shiner is also called the roach or bream. It has a flat, wide body and a small, upturned mouth. The scales are distinct, fairly large and a pale gold in color. It is found from North Dakota to southern Ontario and south to Oklahoma and Arkansas. Another form, the eastern golden shiner *(Notemigonus crysoleucas crysoleucas)* is found from New Brunswick, Quebec and the St. Lawrence River southward, east of the Appalachians, to Virginia. Still another form is found in the southern states. The golden shiners make good bait and may reach 12 inches in length in our northern states and 18 inches in our southern states. They prefer the shallower lakes, ponds and sluggish streams and have been raised successfully in artificial ponds.

NORTHERN COMMON SHINER

(Notropis cornutus frontalis)

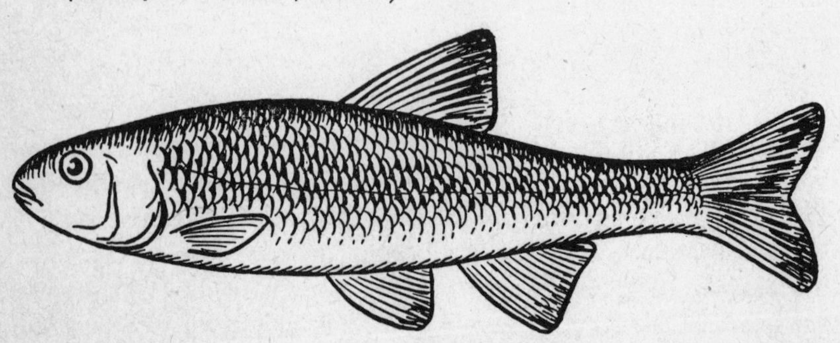

This minnow is also known as the silverside or just plain shiner. It has a steel-blue back, large, silvery scales and white belly. It is found in the cooler creeks and lakes from Canada south to Colorado, Kansas,

Missouri and from the Rockies east to New England. It is a popular bait minnow, but is less hardy than many species. It reaches a maximum length of about 8 inches. Another form, the central common shiner *(Notropis cornutus chrysocephalus)*, is found in the southern Great Lakes area south to Alabama and Oklahoma. There are many other shiners which belong to this same genus, a few of which are the lake emerald shiner, northern redfin shiner, spotfin shiner, river shiner, spottail shiner, blackchin shiner and the northern blacknose shiner. Most of the shiners make attractive bait, although they are more delicate than some of the other minnows.

BRASSY MINNOW
(Hybognathus hankinsoni)

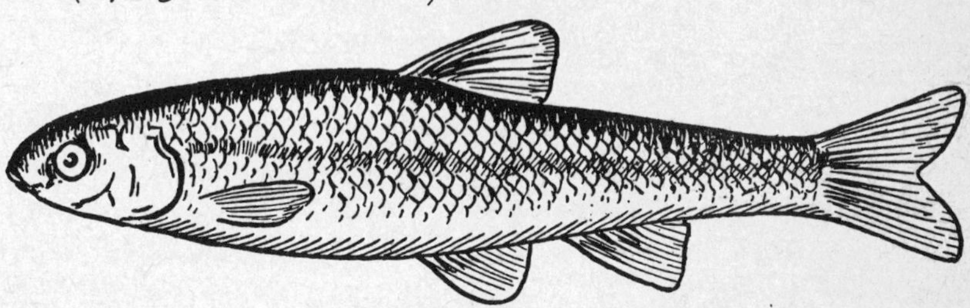

This minnow has a blunt head, small mouth and short, rounded fins. The scales are large, brassy in color along the sides and come off easily. It is found through most of the Great Lakes region and from Montana to southern Ontario southward to Colorado, Nebraska, Iowa and southern Michigan. It prefers small creeks, bog waters and is found occasionally in lakes.

FATHEAD MINNOW
(Pimephales promelas promelas)

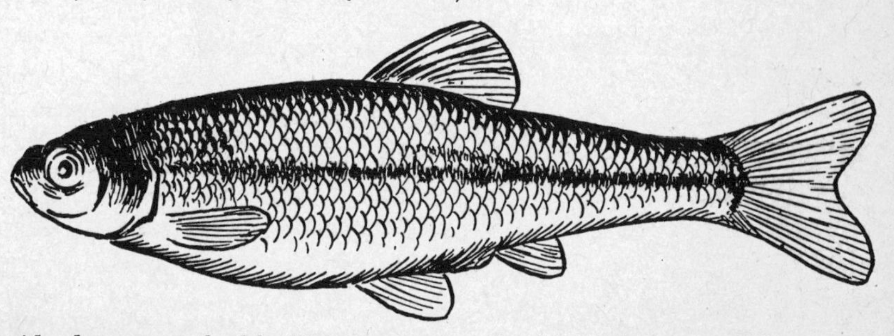

Also known as the blackhead minnow, this bait fish is one of the easiest to raise artificially in small ponds. It is a small minnow reaching

3½ inches in length and has a heavy body, varying in color from olivaceous to black. It is found throughout southern Canada and the northern United States. It prefers small lakes, ponds and silty streams.

BLUNTNOSE MINNOW

(Hyborhynchus notatus)

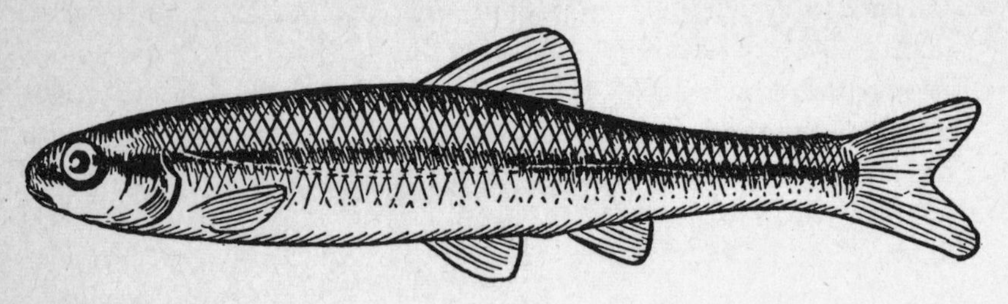

This is another minnow which can well be raised artificially in ponds. It is a long, slim minnow olivaceous silver in color with a dark spot at the base of the tail. It reaches a length of 4 inches. It is found from Winnipeg through the Great Lakes region to Quebec and southward to Virginia and the Gulf States. The bluntnose minnow prefers clear lakes and streams.

CARP AND GOLDFISH

These two members of the minnow family are often used as bait when young, but it is a practice which should be discouraged. In fact, many states prohibit their use. Carp and goldfish are prolific fish and when introduced into lakes and rivers soon crowd out the game fish. They feed on vegetation and root up the mud bottom, dirtying the water and destroying plant life. This usually creates unfavorable conditions for game fish and results in poor fishing. Of course, where carp and goldfish are already present in a lake or river, there can be no harm in using them for bait in the same waters. But they should not be used as bait in strange waters. Check your state laws before using carp or goldfish for bait.

The above list is far from complete and includes only the most popular and common minnows. There are many other species which can be used for bait, but those which are most numerous in your locality are the easiest to obtain and usually make the best bait.

Minnows can be caught in almost any brook, stream, river or lake. The best place to look for them depends on the species present and the formation of the shoreline, depth of water, current and hiding places. Some species will be found in the quiet pools, others in the riffles and still others among the weeds. In lakes, minnows congregate in the shallow coves and near feeder streams emptying into the lake. Piers, docks and spots where table scraps and other food is dumped into the water often attract minnows in large numbers.

CATCHING, KEEPING AND PRESERVING

The most efficient method of obtaining minnows quickly and in large numbers is by means of a seine. But before a seine is used make sure that it is legal in the waters you intend to try. Most states have laws specifying the waters where seining is allowed and also regulate the length, mesh and width of the seine used. Seines from 4 to 100 feet long are used, depending on the body of water and the persons available.

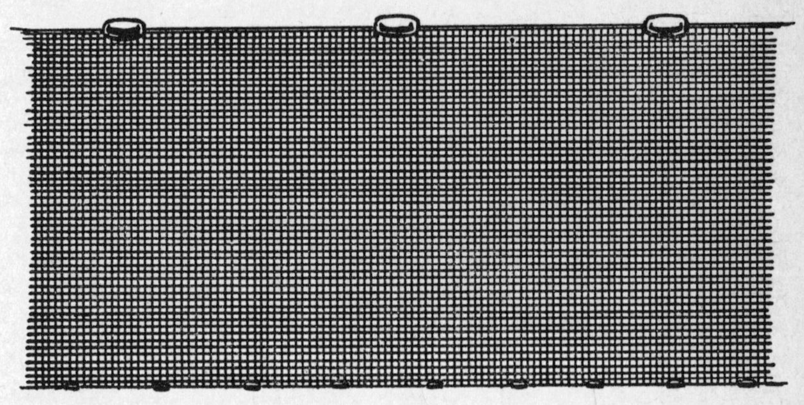

Minnow Seine

The short seines are popular in small brooks, streams and ponds and can be operated by one man. The larger seines are best for rivers and lakes and are operated by two or more men. In shallow water two men can use the seine by wading, and in deeper water two rowboats can draw the seine. The general procedure is to start some distance away from shore and to draw the seine toward land, forming a half-circle so that the two ends of the seine touch land and cut off the escape of the minnows. Another way is to anchor one end on shore and swing the other end around until it touches land.

When the haul has been completed there will be an assorted catch of various sizes of minnows and many other species of water life in the seine. Don't remove the seine from the water to the shore. Form a bag with the seine and float it out to deeper, cleaner water. Then the big minnows which are to be used for bait should be dipped out with a small hand net and placed in the bait pail. The small minnows and other species in the seine should be carefully returned to the water. Too many bait seiners haul the net to shore, pick out the minnows they want and then dump the rest on dry land to perish. This not only destroys valuable minnows, but will also kill any young game fish or pan fish present in the seine, not to mention various water insects and crustaceans which are important fish foods.

Another method used in catching minnows is the "drop" or "umbrella" type net, which is usually square in shape and has lines attached to each corner for lifting. There are many types and designs on the

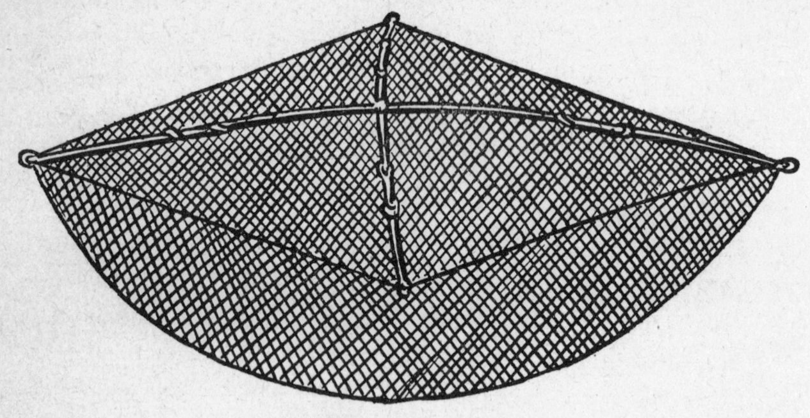

Minnow Drop Net

market which can be bought cheaply. Or you can easily construct one using wire, line, and cheesecloth or mosquito netting. It can be any size from 3 to 10 feet square. The smaller ones are best because they can be worked by hand and do not require supports or pulleys like the larger ones. There are small portable types on the market which have a collapsible frame that takes up little space when folded.

These drop nets are lowered to the bottom in shallow spots or to a depth of a few feet in deeper spots where minnows are known to be plentiful. Then soaked bread, crumbled cracker, or oatmeal is thrown above the net and permitted to sink into it. After the minnows have gathered over the net it can be lifted quickly to catch them.

Still another method widely used for catching minnows is by means of traps. These can be bought in almost any tackle store and come in a variety of shapes, sizes and materials. Most of them are either round or rectangular and are made of wire or glass, but there are others made from plastics or cloth mesh. They all work on the same idea. There are one or more funnel entrances which make it easy for the minnows to enter but hard to escape the trap. The traps are set

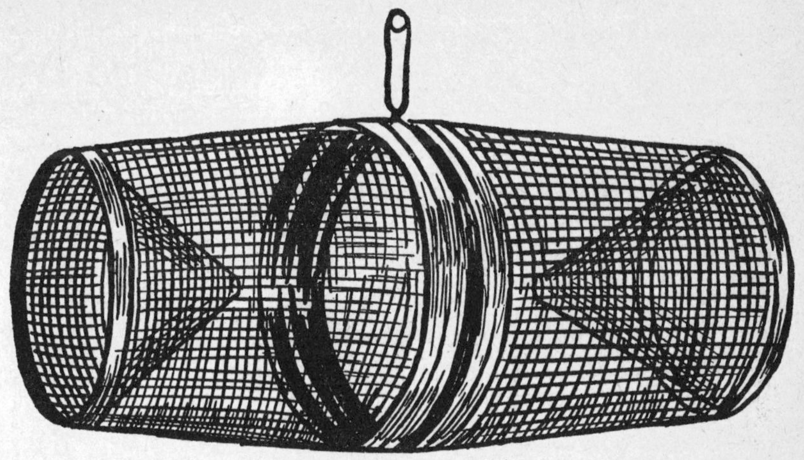

Wire Minnow Trap

in a stream or lake where minnows are plentiful, and are baited with bread or cracker crumbs. In streams the funnel entrance should face downstream and a shallow hole should be dug in the stream bottom to hold the trap. For best results the trap should be examined about every half hour to prevent any minnows from escaping after the food is gone. If you use more than one trap you can catch a good supply of minnows in a short time. Here again, it is best to check your state laws, for some states limit the size and number of traps which can be used.

Some of the larger minnows can be caught on hook and line using small No. 16 or 18 hooks baited with bits of worm or doughball. The doughball bait can easily be made by mixing flour with water and kneading it into dough. Or you can soak some bread and then squeeze out the excess water to make bait. But the hook and line method is a slow one at best and is usually used when only a few extra-large minnows are needed.

Of course, if you can't obtain minnows in any other way, or if you need them in a hurry, you can always buy some from a tackle store, bait dealer or boat livery which carries them. But if you do a lot of fishing with minnows it is cheaper to catch your own bait.

After the minnows are caught, if you are going fishing soon, they can be transferred to a pail or bait bucket. An ordinary pail will sometimes serve, if the weather is cool, to hold minnows for short periods of time and carry them short distances. When you get to the lake or stream you can place the pail in the water in a shady spot just deep enough to submerge it until about three-quarters of the pail is covered.

But if you are traveling long distances or fishing from a boat, a special minnow bucket is much better. There are many types and sizes on the market. The most popular is the metal type holding from 2 to 4 quarts of water. Those having a perforated inner lining which floats in the water are good. Then there are the canvas types which permit oxygen to enter through the walls, and which keep cool through the

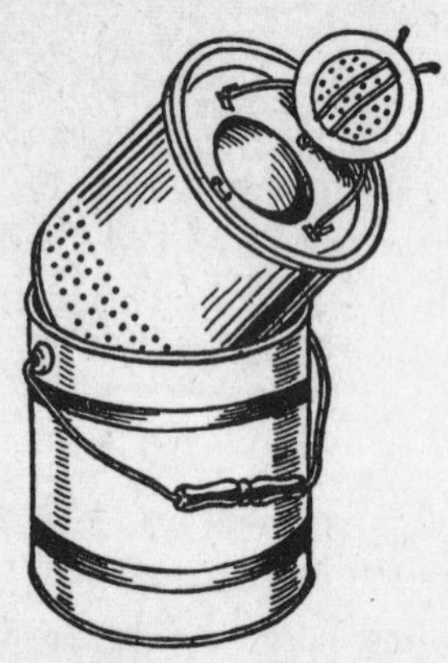

Minnow Bucket

evaporation of moisture on the outside of the container. Many of the metal types have built-in air pumps which keep the minnows supplied with oxygen.

The important things to remember in handling, transporting and keeping minnows is not to crowd them, and to keep the water cool and rich in oxygen. Also, when transferring minnows from one container to another, make sure that the water temperature in the new container is nearly the same as in the one from which they came.

For short trips the water can often be aerated by dipping up some of it from the minnow bucket with a dipper and pouring it back from a height several times during the trip. For longer trips and in hot weather you can place ice on top of the minnow bucket and allow it to drip into the container as it melts. Or you can place the minnow bucket in a box or tub and surround it with cracked ice. A tire pump can also be used to aerate the water.

To keep minnows in large numbers for future use you will need large tanks or small pools which have a constant supply of cool, well-aerated water entering under pressure from above the water level. The drain or outlet should be near the bottom of such a tank or pool to permit stagnant water and wastes to leave. City water or any other water with too much chlorine should not be used unless the excess chlorine is removed by aeration or filters.

Minnows can also be kept for long periods of time in live boxes. Such a box can easily be made to accommodate a good supply of minnows. Don't make it too small or too large, however. The minnows thrive better if they have plenty of room, but too large a box, on the other hand is heavy and unwieldy. One about 26 inches in length, 20 inches in width and about 12 inches high is a good size. Build the wooden frame this size, then cut boards to cover the top of the box and nail them in place. Now cut out a door in the center of this wooden top and fasten it on with a pair of hinges. Cover the rest of the frame with quarter-inch wire mesh on all sides and the box is ready for use.

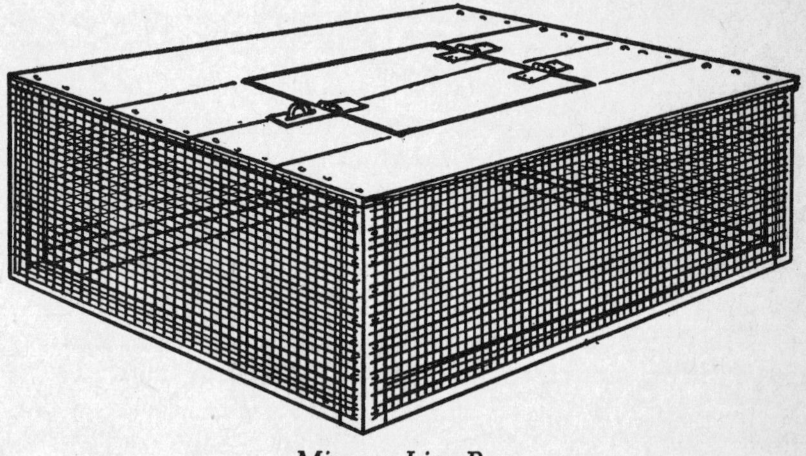

Minnow Live Box

If the water in the lake or stream is cool and flowing the live box can be kept close to shore. But if the water is warm or rough, minnows will live better if you sink the box in deep water where it is cooler, cleaner and there is no wave action to toss the minnows around.

Springs are usually good places to keep minnows since the water is clean and cool during the summer months, while during the winter it doesn't freeze too readily and enables the angler to keep minnows to be used for ice-fishing.

When keeping minnows for any length of time it is best to keep those of approximately the same size together in the same tank. If you are keeping minnows only for a few days there is no need to feed them, but if they are being held more than a week or so you should feed them once every two or three days to keep them healthy. Some of the foods used for minnows include oatmeal, bread, corn meal, crackers, finely ground meat and fish and various commercial preparations. It is important not to overfeed the minnows because the leftover food will decay and contaminate the water.

To keep minnows free from disease they should not be overcrowded or handled roughly. If the film which covers the fish is removed or the skin is broken by careless handling the minnows may become infected by bacteria or fungus. The fungus shows up as a white fuzz on various parts of the body and spreads all over until the minnow dies. It occurs most often when the water is warm. As soon as any minnow develops this fungus it should be removed from the tank or live box and placed in a different container, where you can try to treat it. One solution which is recommended is 1/8 ounce of malachite green in 15 gallons of water. The minnow should be dipped in this solution for ten seconds. This treatment can also be given to healthy minnows which have been exposed to the disease in order to prevent the fungus infection.

Another disease in minnows is fin rot, which is caused by bacteria of several kinds. In this disease the fins or tail of the minnows degenerate until they are entirely destroyed. To control this disease dip the sick minnows in a solution of copper sulphate containing 6.5 ounces to 100 gallons of water for one or two minutes. Another solution recommended for this disease is made of formalin, using 8 ounces to 100 gallons of water, and the minnows are kept in this for one hour. If the disease has progressed too far, however, these dips will not help much and the minnows should be destroyed.

One of the best ways to prevent diseases is to sterilize, at regular intervals, the tank or box in which minnows are kept. This can be done by scrubbing the containers with a solution of 1 quart of sodium hypochlorite to 250 gallons of water. Rinse the containers with fresh water to remove all traces of the solution before you put any minnows into them.

Although live minnows are generally best for fishing, there are times when minnows are scarce or hard to obtain and dead or preserved minnows must be used. For certain kinds of fishing, like trolling and casting and retrieving, dead minnows often serve just as well as live ones. Many anglers would like to know how minnows can be preserved for future use.

Minnows can be kept for a few days by placing them in layers in a container and covering each layer with salt. Although they will turn hard and shrivel somewhat, as soon as they are used in the water they will soften up again. Minnows can also be kept for a few weeks in a jar with strong brine. However, the best method of keeping minnows indefinitely requires the use of formaldehyde. One formula calls for a solution of one percent formalin and 99 percent water and an airtight jar. A mayonnaise or Mason jar will do. The minnows are killed and placed in this solution. Seal the jar and watch the solution inside for any signs of discoloring. When this happens make up a fresh solution and, after washing the minnows, place them in it. If you find the minnows are too stiff, you should use less formalin; if they are too soft you can add more formalin. You may have to change the solution two or three times before it remains clear. Some anglers add from 5 to 10 percent glycerin to keep the minnows soft.

Another method of preserving minnows which helps to eliminate the objectionable formalin odor calls for one part formalin, 6 parts glycerin and 40 parts water. The minnows are kept in this solution from four to six weeks and then are removed and transferred to a strong brine which will remove the formalin odor. Other anglers keep the minnows in a formalin solution but add a few drops of rhodium oil to kill the odor.

METHODS OF HOOKING

Minnows can be used for trout, black bass, walleyes, lake trout, pike, pickerel, muskellunge and many other game fish. They will also take pan fish like crappies, yellow perch, white perch, white bass, sunfish and even coarse fish like catfish and eels. The size of the minnow used depends on the fish being sought. Minnows from 1½ to 2½ inches are best for pan fish. Trout minnows usually run from 2 to 3 inches. For bass the minnows can run from 2½ to 5 inches, while for pike and muskellunge minnows from 4 to 10 inches are not too big. If you are looking only for big fish it is best to use the larger minnows. But if you want as much action as possible use the smaller ones, for a big fish will often take a small minnow, but it is difficult for a small fish to mouth a large minnow.

There are many ways of hooking a minnow, depending on the fish sought, the water being fished and the method of angling being used. For still-fishing, minnows are usually hooked through the back, side or belly. The most popular way is to run the hook through the back just in front or behind the dorsal fin, being careful not to strike

Hooking for Still Fishing and Casting

the backbone. This method is good if the minnow is just being lowered into the water or is being cast out only a few feet. For making longer casts, hooking through both lips is much better.

Several other methods are used in hooking minnows for casting and trolling. One simple method is to run the point and barb of the hook into the minnow's mouth, then out through one of the gill openings and into the back behind the dorsal fin. Another method calls for the use of two hooks with one of them tied to the leader or snell about two inches above the other. Then one hook is run through the minnow's lips while the end hook is inserted into the minnow's back, near the tail. In both these methods a slight bend can be produced so that it spins when retrieved, drifted or trolled.

Hooking with Double Hook

Another method calls for the use of a double hook. A large needle is needed to pull the leader end through the minnow's mouth and out of the vent. Then a double hook is tied to the end of the leader and the shank is pulled into the bait's body. The minnow's body rests between the two hooks, the points of which face upwards. There's a variation of this method which calls for the double hook at the head of the minnow. Here the needle to which the leader end is tied is first inserted into the vent and pushed through the minnow's body until it emerges from its mouth. A double hook is attached to the leader end, then the shank is pulled back into the bait's mouth causing the head of the minnow to rest between the two hooks.

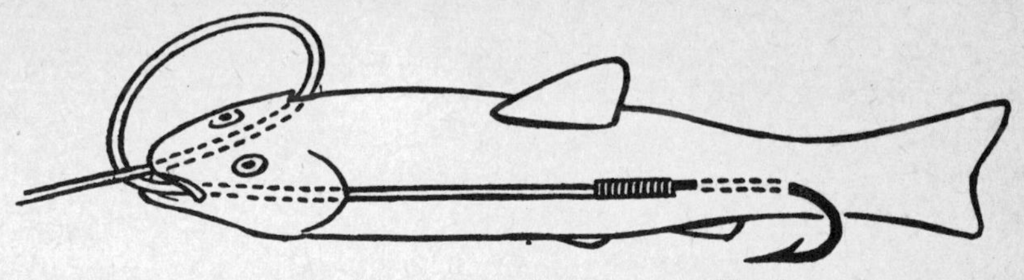

Method of Sewing Minnow on Hook

Still another headfirst method can be worked out with a single hook by sewing the minnow on the hook and leader. Here the entire hook is pushed through the minnow just above the tail and a few inches of the leader is pulled through. Then the leader is wrapped completely around the minnow and the hook is forced through the body again under the forward part of the dorsal fin, after which the point of the hook is worked through the bait's gills and out of its mouth. Finally the slack in the leader is tightened up until the bend of the hook rests against the minnow's mouth with the point clearing the head enough to hook a striking fish.

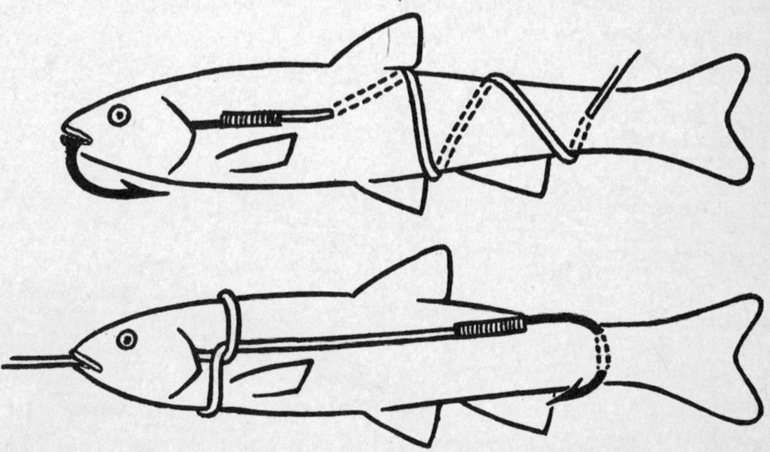

Two Ways To Sew a Minnow on the Hook

In rigging a minnow so that it will have a permanent bend which will cause it to spin or wobble when moved through the water, each angler has his own pet method. One of the simplest is to run your hook into the minnow's mouth and out of the gill opening. Then tie a half hitch around the minnow's body just back of the head and insert the hook about midway between the dorsal fin and the tail. Finally you tighten up on the leader, putting a bend into the minnow, and secure the half hitch. Another way to get this permanent bend is to run your hook into the minnow's mouth and out of the gill opening and pull through about four inches of leader. Then run the hook into the minnow's mouth a second time and out through the opposite gill opening. Next you insert the hook into the minnow's body along the side near the tail and bring it out on the same side. Now pull on the leader against the hook, creating in the minnow the bend that you want. Tighten up on the slack leader loop alongside the bait's head to keep the bend in place.

There are also many types of minnow gangs on the market which hold the minnow in place and these can be bought in most tackle stores. Some have spinners attached to give them an added attraction. The thing to remember when using minnows is that movement and flash attract game fish, and this must be brought about by the activities of the live minnow itself or the manipulation of a dead minnow by the current or the angler.

Chapter III

OTHER BAIT FISHES

THIS SECTION INCLUDES ALL THE FISHES WHICH ARE NOT TRUE MINNOWS but which are often used for bait. Many of the methods of capturing, keeping and transporting minnows, dealt with in the previous section, can be applied to the fishes in this group. Likewise the methods described for hooking minnows are also suitable for most of these fishes.

SUCKERS

The sucker family is a large one with some 100 species found in North America. They are closely related to the minnows and are often mis-

Common White Sucker

taken for them when young. However, most of them can be recognized by the thick, fleshy lips and by the 10 or more rays in the dorsal fin. They live on the bottom in lakes, rivers and streams. Most of them ascend smaller streams and brooks to spawn in the spring. One of the most widely distributed species is the common white sucker (*Catostomus commersonii commersonii*) which is found east of the Great Plains from Canada to Georgia. Some of the other suckers are the sturgeon suckers, the hog sucker, the spotted sucker and the chub suckers. The sucker family also includes the buffalo fishes, the quillbacks and the red horses. The buffalo fishes may reach 3 feet in length and a weight of 60 pounds, and some of the other suckers will often go several pounds. But only the young ones from about 3 to 10 inches are used for bait. The 6 to 10 inch suckers make good pike and muskellunge baits. Some of the larger suckers can be caught on hook and line, but most of them are taken in traps and seines.

STONE CATS, MAD TOMS AND BULLHEADS

Stone Cat

Northern Black Bullhead

These small members of the catfish family are used as bait for many game fish and are especially popular for black bass. The stone cats and mad toms can be recognized by their small size and by the fact that the adipose fin is continuous along the back and joins with the tail fin. In the other catfishes the adipose fin and tail or caudal fins are separated. The stone cat (*Noturus flavus*) is one of the larger members and may reach 10 or 12 inches. It is found east of the Rockies, from Canada south to Virginia and Texas. The mad toms, which belong to the genera *Schilbeodes*, usually run from 3 to 5 inches and there are several species such as the tadpole mad tom, freckled mad tom, common eastern mad tom, slender mad tom, brindled mad tom and mountain mad tom. Most of these small catfishes are found in the riffles under stones in creeks and rivers, although some prefer the quieter water with weeds. They can be caught in the shallow water by striking flat stones with another rock to stun the fish, and when the rock is turned over they can be picked up with a small dip net. After they are put in a bait pail they will revive in a short time. Care should be taken in handling these stone cats and mad toms, for their sharp spines have poison glands at the base which can cause a painful wound.

The bullheads, which grow larger than the stone cats and mad toms, can be used for bait when young (from 2 to 5 inches in length) for black bass, walleyed pike and other game fish. They are also used (from 5 to 10 inches) for the larger catfishes, especially on set or trot lines which remain in the water a long time. When using them for game fish it is often a good idea to clip off the sharp spines in the fins to make the bait more attractive and easier to swallow. Three species, the black bullhead, the brown bullhead and the yellow bullhead are commonly found in many parts of the country. The bullheads prefer the quieter streams, rivers and ponds, and lakes with muddy, weedy bottoms where they can be caught on hook and line using worms for bait. They are especially active at night and when the water is muddy from recent rains. The stone cats, mad toms and bullheads are very hardy baits and will live for a long time in bait pails, tanks or on the hook. Several fish can often be caught on one bait.

LAMPREYS

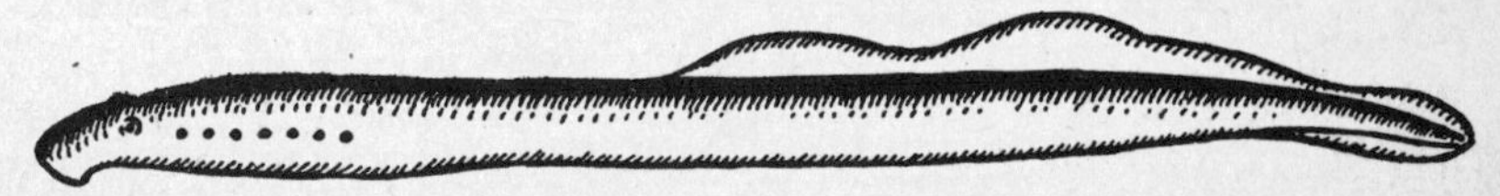

American Brook Lamprey

Although lampreys look like eels and are often called "lamprey eels," they are not related to eels at all but fall into a special primitive class lower than the other fishes. The true eels have jaws, while the lampreys have a circular funnel-shaped mouth lined with horny spines. This round sucking mouth fastens on to the side of a fish and rasps a hole through which nourishment is obtained. Not all of the several species of lampreys are parasitic and harmful to fishes, but one of the most destructive is the sea lamprey, which may reach 2 or 3 feet and is really a salt-water species. It lives along the Atlantic Coast but ascends rivers to spawn. It has become landlocked in some lakes where it causes great damage to fresh-water fishes. Two other lampreys which are strictly fresh-water species but are also harmful to fishes are the silver lamprey and the chestnut lamprey. Two harmless species are the Michigan brook lamprey and the American brook lamprey.

Lampreys make good bait for game fish and are especially favored for black bass and walleyes. But because of the harmful habits of the parasitic lampreys they should not be used for bait in waters where they are not already present—this to prevent their spreading. Lampreys which are used for bait are found buried in mud bottoms of streams and rivers. To obtain them, dig in a few inches of water near shore, dumping the mud on the bank, and then look through the mud for the lampreys. They make a tough, but slippery bait and are often used behind a spinner for walleyes. They will also take sturgeon occasionally in some of the rivers when fished on the bottom. To hook them, run the hook through one of the holes or gill openings just behind the head and let the point come out through the opposite side.

DARTERS

Northern Log Perch

These small fishes look like minnows but belong to the perch family. They have a long, slim body and the males are brightly colored during the spawning season. They lie on the bottoms of streams or lakes, resting on their large pectoral fins. When disturbed they dart forward a short distance and come to rest on the bottom again. In size they usually range from 1 to 8 inches but average from about 2 to 4 inches. One of the most popular darters used for bait is the northern log perch (*Percina caprodes semifasciata*) which is also known as the sand pike, stone pike, and zebra fish. It is found in many parts of Canada and from Minnesota to Vermont. The Ohio log perch (*Percina caprodes caprodes*), a closely related form, is found farther south. There are many other kinds of darters found in various parts of the country and many of them can be used for bait. Although they are somewhat dark in color and do not live too well in tanks, they are hardy on the hook. They can be caught on hook and line using tiny hooks and bits of worms as bait. Black bass, pike and other game fish will take them.

YELLOW PERCH

Small yellow perch are sometimes used as bait for fish like black bass, walleyes, pike and muskellunge. Some anglers cut off the sharp dorsal fin to make the bait more attractive. An old favorite lure used in skittering for pickerel is a strip cut from a perch's belly leaving the two ventral fins attached. If you run out of bait while pan fishing you can cut up a yellow perch into small cubes and use them to catch other yellow perch, crappies and sunfish. Even the eye of a perch can often be used as bait. But this is another bait which should be used with care, since perch have ruined many a stream and lake when introduced by accident or deliberately. Such waters have often become overpopulated with stunted yellow perch, resulting in a depletion of game fish. Of course, where yellow perch are already present it is safe to use them as bait, but check your state laws to see if it is legal.

SUNFISH

Small sunfish will sometimes take black bass, pike and muskellunge. They also make a good bait for big catfish fished on or near the bottom. Sunfish used for game fish must be quite small, however, since their width makes them difficult for the fish to swallow. Cutting off the sharp spines of the dorsal fin will make them more attractive baits. There are many species of sunfishes and most of them can be used for bait.

ALEWIFE AND GIZZARD SHAD

These members of the herring family are occasionally used as bait although they are delicate and do not stay alive too long on the hook or in a tank. The alewife (*Pomolobus pseudoharengus*) is really a saltwater species but ascends fresh-water streams and rivers along the Atlantic Coast to spawn. In some of the lakes, however, they are landlocked. The alewife has a deep, flat body and may reach 6 inches in length. The gizzard shad (*Dorosoma cepedianum*) also has a deep, compressed body but it can easily be recognized by the long, thin last

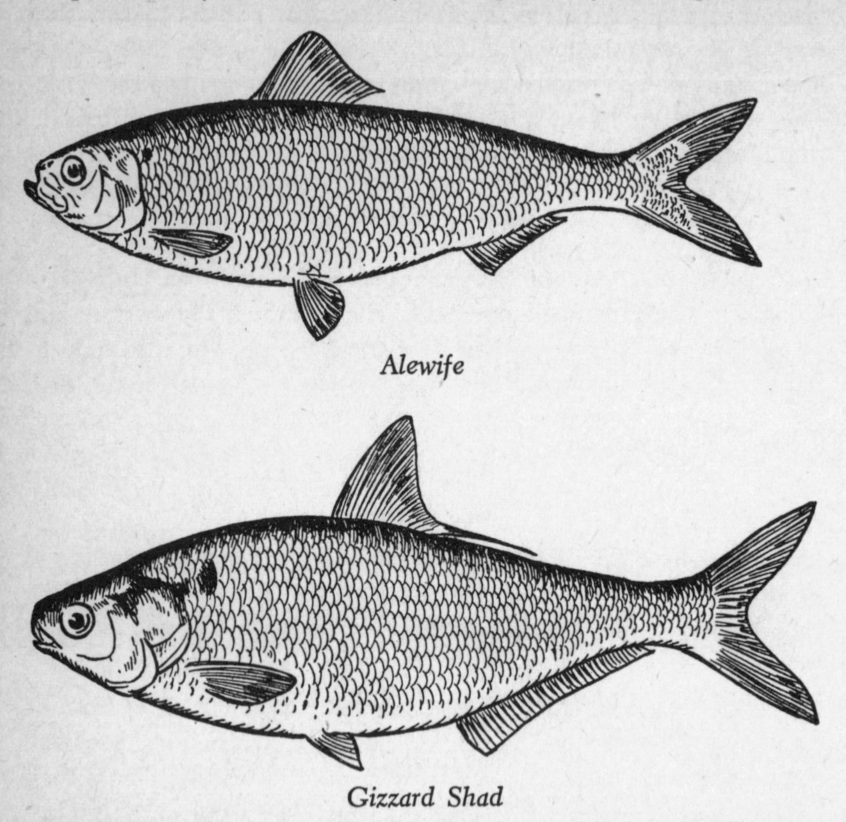

Alewife

Gizzard Shad

ray of the dorsal fin. It is found in large bodies of water from Minnesota to New York and southward to Mexico and the Gulf Coast. It becomes very numerous in man-made lakes and reservoirs, and serves as an important food supply for the game fishes. It may reach up to 16 inches in length but the average is much smaller.

KILLIFISHES

These small fishes include many species, some of which are found in fresh water while others frequent brackish and salt water. The fresh-water species include the eastern banded killifish, the western banded killifish, the northern starhead top minnow, and the blackstripe top minnow. The common killifish or mummichog (*Fundulus heteroclitus*) is a brackish or salt-water species which is found along the Atlantic Coast and the Gulf of Mexico. The reason it is included here is that it is readily taken by many fresh-water game fish and is one of the hardiest bait fishes an angler can use. It will live for a long time when packed in cool, damp seaweed, moss or grass. Because of this, and

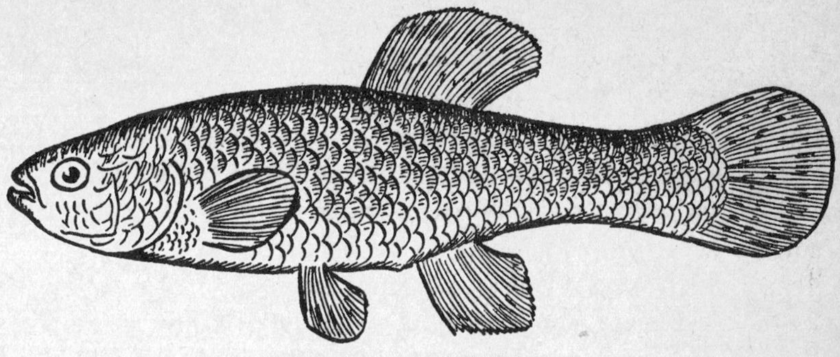

Common Killifish

since it lives well on a hook, the mummichog is used often despite the fact that killifish in general are rather dark and dull in coloring. They grow up to 5 or 6 inches in length although the average found will be between 1½ and 3 inches.

THE SCULPINS OR MUDDLERS

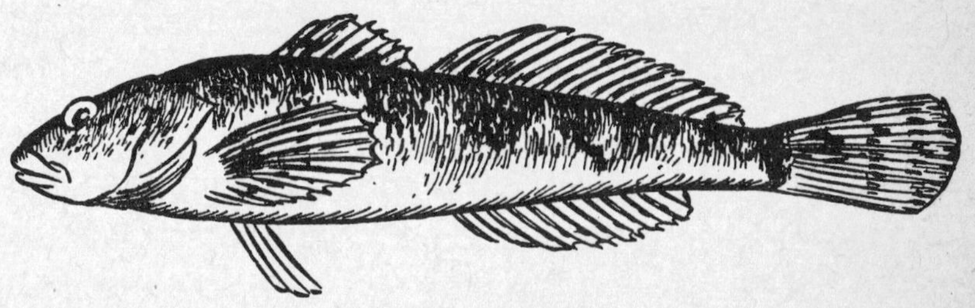

Northern Muddler

These small bottom-dwelling fish with large, flattened heads and wing-like pectoral fins are sometimes used as bait. They are rather drab in color and usually try to hide under a stone or in the weeds when on a hook. But they are hardy baits and are often effective for big trout and other game fish. There are several species of sculpins and one of the most popular is the northern muddler (*Cottus bairdii bairdii*) which is also called the common sculpin and miller's-thumb. It is usually found in streams but also lives in lakes with boulder-lined shores. The muddlers usually remain hidden during the daytime under stones and can be caught at night in the shallow riffles by using a flashlight and dip net. During the daytime they can often be caught by turning over the stones in narrow, shallow riffles and chasing them downstream into a scoop trap made from wire screening.

There are quite a few other small fishes used as bait at times. The mudsucker or long-jawed goby (*Gillichthys mirabilis*) is a small Pacific Coast salt-water fish which is popular with fresh-water anglers. The common eel is often cut up and used as bait for big catfish, while the young eels can be used for many game fish. The smelt is used for lake trout and other game fish. The mud minnow (*Umbra limi*) is a hardy bait which will live a long time on the hook.

And finally strips cut from almost any large fish including the game fishes themselves can often be used as bait. These are usually cut from the belly into a variety of sizes and shapes to suit the type of fishing being done and the fish sought. In general, though, the longer and narrower the strip the more action it has when moved through the water. Another bait which can be used is the eye of practically any fish. Fish are more or less cannibalistic and the eye of a brook trout, for example, has been gouged out and used to catch other brook trout.

Of course, it is impossible in a book of this sort to include every fish that is used for bait. There are many bait fishes which are only of local importance, being found in limited areas and used only by the natives in that spot. And local fishing conditions can make a bait deadly in one area and practically useless in another. When fishing strange waters you can't go wrong by listening to the advice offered by the local anglers and bait and tackle dealers.

Chapter IV

WATER INSECTS

INSECTS WHICH SPEND MOST OR PART OF THEIR LIVES IN THE WATER are eaten by many fresh-water fishes. Some water insects are so small that they are eaten only by minnows and young game fish, and are too small to use as bait, but others are large enough to interest the bigger fishes and these often make excellent baits.

Insects go through three or four distinct stages of development from the egg to the adult. The immature water insects known as "nymphs" are in the second of three stages: egg—nymph—adult. They resemble the adult insect in the shape and hardness of their bodies. The immature stages of dragonflies, damsel flies, May flies and stone flies are called nymphs. The immature water insects known as "larvae" go through four stages of development: egg—larva—pupa—adult. The larvae do not resemble the adult very much and have soft bodies. The immature stages of caddis flies, hellgrammites or dobson flies, and the true flies are called larvae.

Water insects differ so much in size, structure and habits that general rules cannot be laid down for obtaining, keeping and hooking them. Some are delicate, while others are hardy. Some insects live in clear, running water, while others prefer stagnant, quiet waters. Some live under stones or logs, while others are found in the mud or among water plants. These individual characteristics and habits will be dealt with in the sections below.

There are two devices which can be used to catch many of the water insects. One is a section of wire screening 2 or 3 feet square reinforced by a wooden frame. An old window screen will serve the purpose nicely. The other is a small dip net made from cloth with a fine mesh.

HELLGRAMMITES

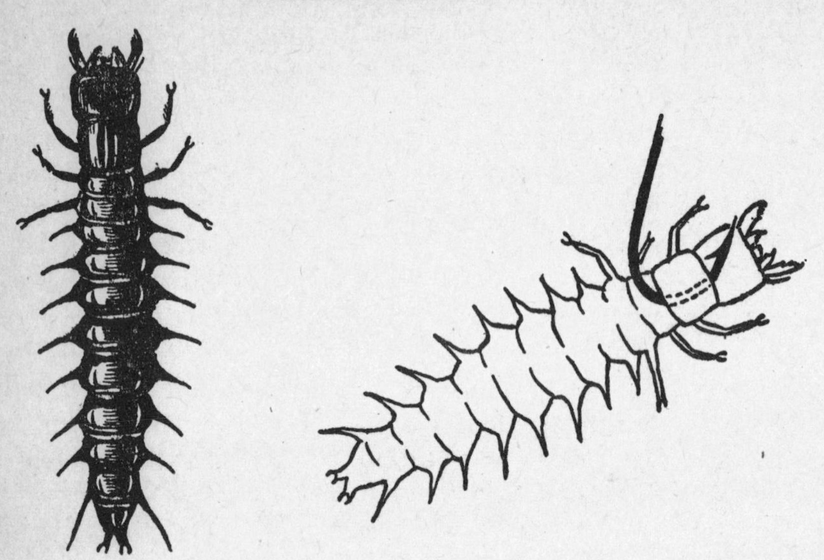

Hellgrammite and Method of Hooking

The hellgrammite (*Corydalis cornutus*) is one of the most popular water insects used for bait. There are quite a few insects called hellgrammites, but this is the true one and it is the larval form of the big, winged insect known as the dobson fly. Hellgrammites are known by different names in various parts of the country—alligator, water grampus, conniption bug, helldiver, snipper, clipper, flip-flap, crawler and many others.

The adult dobson fly is a big insect with a wingspread of 4 inches. The female fly lays several thousand eggs on branches, rocks or other objects overhanging a stream. When the eggs hatch, the tiny larvae drop into the water and live there for nearly three years, hiding under the rocks in the rapids or riffles and feeding on other water insects. When the hellgrammite is fully grown (at two years and 11 months) it crawls out on land, hides under a log or stone for about a month and transforms into the adult dobson fly. Then the cycle is repeated all over again.

A fully grown hellgrammite may reach 3 inches in length, but most of those found in streams will run from 1 to 2½ inches. It is a long, black or dark brown creature with 6 legs and a pair of appendages on each segment of its soft body. It also has a pair of nippers which can inflict a painful bite, and two tiny hooks on the end of the tail section. Hellgrammites are most numerous in the fast water of streams and rivers, where they can be caught by turning over the rocks while a wire screen or net is held below the rocks. Although one man can easily hold the screen with one hand and lift rocks with the other, two people are better. Then one man can turn over several rocks at a time while his companion holds the screen below them. The fast current will sweep the hellgrammites onto the screen where they will hang on for a short while. It also pays to examine each stone you lift to see if any hellgrammites are clinging to it.

Hellgrammites can be kept for a long time in running water and fed ground meat to prevent cannibalism. They will also live for weeks in a cool cellar in a box or other container having decayed leaves or rotten logs. These should be kept damp but not too wet. Small containers or bait boxes filled with leaves, grass or weeds can be used to carry hellgrammites when fishing. They will live all day if you keep the container out of the sun and sprinkle the leaves with water occasionally.

The hellgrammite is a tough bait which will stay alive on a hook for a long time. You can often catch several fish on one bait. The best way to hook hellgrammites is to run the hook under the hard collar just behind the head. Some anglers break off the two tiny hooks at the end of the tail so that the bait cannot grasp the bottom and hide under a rock or log. They can also be hooked through the tail. Hellgrammites are good for black bass, especially the smallmouth bass found in rivers and streams. They will take trout in some waters and also walleyes, sunfish, yellow perch, rock bass and other pan fish.

The larva of another insect, closely related to the hellgrammite, resembles it somewhat. It is known as the fish fly (*Chauliodes pectinicornis*). But it doesn't reach the size of the hellgrammite and prefers quieter waters where it lives among water plants on the bottom. It can also be used as bait for many of the same fishes which take the hellgrammite.

DRAGONFLIES AND DAMSEL FLIES

These insects are readily recognized in the adult stage when they are seen flying over the water. The dragonfly is especially noticeable and is called by many names, such as darning needle, mule killer, snake doc-

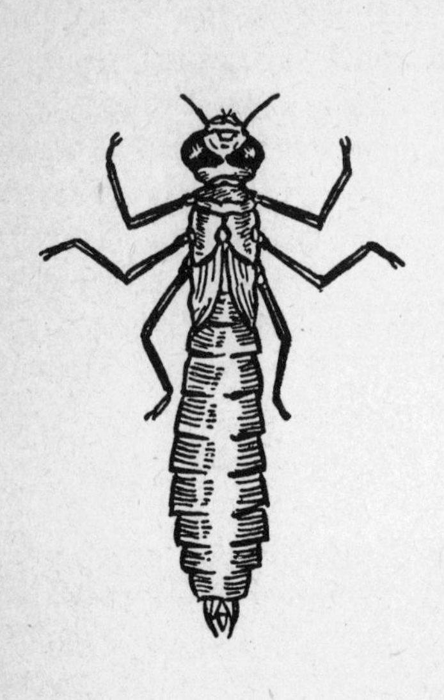

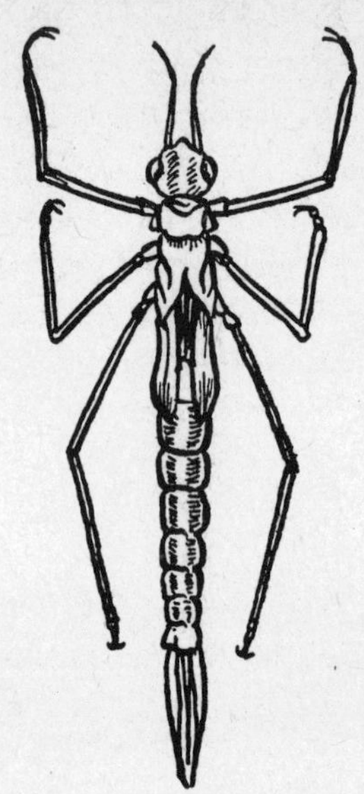

Dragonfly Nymph. Damsel Fly Nymph

tor and snake feeder. Although they look somewhat alike, the dragonfly is not as delicate as the damsel fly, and holds its wings at right angles to the body when at rest. The damsel fly folds its wings vertically and holds them at an angle over the abdomen. There are many different species of dragonflies and damsel flies in this country and they vary in coloring and size.

But it is the nymphs of the dragonflies and damsel flies which we are interested in and these are eaten by many fresh-water fishes. The dragonfly nymphs have broad, flat bodies and the abdomen is usually wider than the head. The damsel fly nymphs have long, thin bodies and the abdomen is usually narrower than the head.

Dragonfly nymphs are called "Perch bugs" and "bass bugs" in various parts of the country. They live in ponds, lakes and the quieter sections of streams in the mud, vegetation and debris. They usually crawl very slowly using their legs, but can shoot forward fast by expelling water from the tail end of their bodies. The nymphs spend from 1 to 3 or more years in the water feeding on other water insects. When they are fully grown they crawl out of the water up a plant stem, rock or tree, where the insect splits down the back and emerges from the skin head first. In the beginning it is very soft, but in less than an hour the wings and body harden and it flies away to spend the rest of its life catching insects on the wing and laying eggs in the water—from which tiny dragonfly nymphs will hatch to repeat the cycle.

The dragonfly and damsel fly nymphs can be caught with seines and dip nets dragged through the plants growing in the water. Or you can use a rake to bring up the debris found on the bottom and search through it for the nymphs. Dragonfly nymphs can be kept in tanks filled with water, but nymphs of about the same size should be kept in the same container, since they are cannibalistic and will eat each other. They can be carried on a fishing trip in containers filled with wet moss or leaves. Dragonfly and damsel fly nymphs are taken by trout, black bass, yellow perch and other pan fish.

CADDIS FLIES

These small insects resemble moths in the adult stage, but have tiny hairs on their wings instead of scales as the true moths do. It is their larvae which are used as bait and are known as stickbaits, stickworms, reedamites, caseworms, barnacle, caddis worms and caddis creepers depending on the kind of case they make and where they are found. For

Caddis Case With Larva and Methods of Hooking

there are a great many species of caddis flies found in the streams and lakes of the country. Each species builds a special kind of case. Some use tiny sticks, stones, sand or leaves which they cement together with a secretion from their mouths. The larva or worm is a whitish-looking grub with six legs and a dark head which builds the case around itself for protection. Those with portable cases drag them around when moving from one place to another. But others build stationary cases which are firmly attached to rocks. Caddis larvae feed on vegetation and animal matter and those species which are the largest in size make the best baits. They can be found in the quieter sections of streams and the weedy shorelines of lakes. If you watch the bottom of the stream or lake closely you can usually spot the caddis larvae crawling very slowly around on the bottom or among the vegetation. They can easily be picked up.

The caddis larvae can be kept in a tank or aquarium if the water is cold. If the water is warm or the tank is overcrowded with the larvae it should be well aerated. Caddis worms tend to be cannibalistic in captivity, so it is better to catch a fresh supply instead of trying to keep them for any length of time. They will live for quite a while in a container filled with wet moss or leaves.

Caddis larvae are a favorite food of trout, which eat them together with the case. They can also be used for bluegills, perch and other pan fish. Although fish eat them case and all, they make more attractive bait if they are removed from their protective covering. This can easily be done by splitting open the case or using a pin or point of a hook to pick out the small worm. To hook one, you can use a small, short shank hook and thread the larvae on, covering the bend and allowing the point to protrude slightly from the head of the bait. Sometimes 2, 3 or 4 caddis worms impaled on a single hook bring more strikes than a single larvae.

MAY FLIES

These delicate insects are eaten by many fresh-water fishes both as adults and nymphs. The adults are easily recognized by the 2 pairs of delicate, net-veined wings, the 3 pairs of long legs, slim abdomen and 2 or 3 long, hairlike tails. Trout fishermen who imitate the May flies when tying dry flies know the adults as shad flies, fish flies and drakes.

However, it is the immature or nymphal stage of the May fly which is used as bait. There are many species of May flies found in the streams, ponds, creeks and lakes of the country. The nymphs vary widely in size and shape. Some prefer the clear, rocky streams where they cling to the stones in riffles. Others burrow in the silt and mud of streams and lakes. Still others swim around freely in the shallows. Most of the May fly nymphs are too small and delicate to make practical baits, but some of them reach a very good size and these can be used.

One of the largest is the nymph of the burrowing May fly which is

May Fly Nymph

often called a "wriggler" or "seahorse." There are several kinds of burrowing May fly nymphs and some reach close to 2 inches in length. They can be recognized by their jaws which have 2 pointed tusks, the

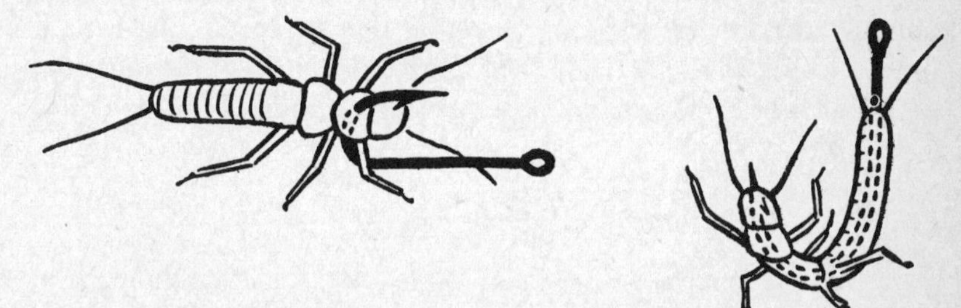

Two Ways To Hook Nymphs

6 pairs of large, bushy gills along the abdomen, and the 3 fuzzy tails. These nymphs live in mud which is slightly porous in depths from a few inches to 40 feet of water. But they are most numerous in water from about 2 to 10 feet in depth. Where they are plentiful you can notice their burrow openings or "blow holes" in the mud bottom. The mud can be scooped up with a shovel and washed out in a small box with a wire-screen bottom to get the nymphs. Some anglers make a special combination shovel and bucket out of ⅛ or ¼ inch mesh of wire screen attached to a long handle. They scoop up the mud, slosh it around in the water to leave the insects exposed for the picking. You can also buy

these nymphs from bait dealers in some areas. They are very popular for bluegills when fishing through the ice in the winter. May fly nymphs can also be used for trout, crappies, perch and other pan fish.

The nymphs can be kept in tanks of cold, well-aerated water. The bottom of the tank should be lined with dead leaves, leaf mold or moss to allow the nymphs to hide. They can be transported to the fishing grounds in damp moss if the weather is cool.

STONE FLIES

Although at first glance the stone fly nymph resembles the May fly nymph, there are differences. The stone fly nymph is flat and has 2 tails instead of the 3 usually found on May fly nymphs. The stone fly nymphs also have longer antennae protruding from the head than the May fly nymphs. The stone fly nymphs usually prefer the fast-running streams where they can be found clinging to the undersides of stones. They vary in size depending on the species, but some of the larger ones can be used for bait. They can easily be gathered by lifting stones from the fast-running water and examining the undersides. These nymphs are often called "hellgrammites," but this tends to confuse them with the true hellgrammite of the dobson fly. They can be kept in cold, running water for future use.

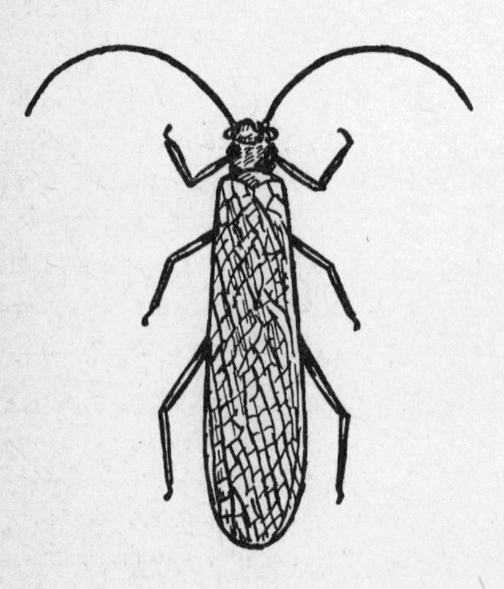

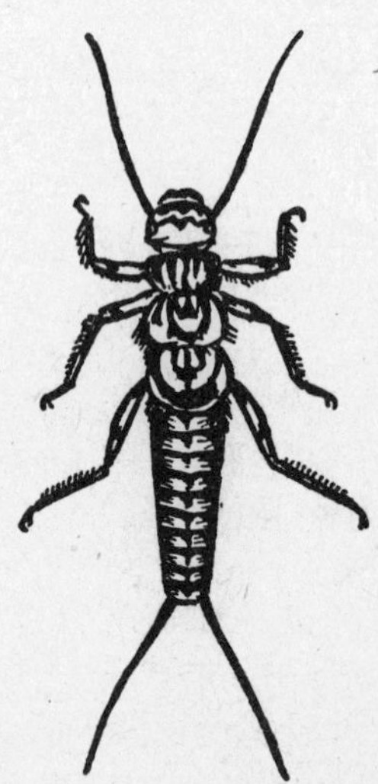

Stone Fly

The adult stone flies resemble the nymphs in body shape and structure but they also have cellophanelike wings which fold flat in a horizontal position over the body. They are poor fliers and are usually seen crawling over the rocks and weeds along the shore of streams. They can also be used as bait for trout being fished on or near the surface. But it is the nymph which is most widely used as bait for trout. They have also been used for whitefish.

For hooking stone fly nymphs, small, fine wire hooks should be used. The nymph can be hooked through the collar just behind the head. Another method is to thread the nymph tail first on a short shanked hook, following the curve of the hook and allowing the point and barb to penetrate to the head of the nymph.

CRANE FLIES

There are many species of these delicate flies which look like overgrown mosquitoes and are often called "daddy-longlegs" and "gallinippers." They do not bite like mosquitoes do and are too fragile to be of any use as bait. But their larvae which looks like an overgrown, translucent maggot is often used as bait. These are also called "leatherjackets" and "waterworms." Some of the larger ones may reach almost 2

Crane Fly Larva

inches in length. They may be brown, white or greenish in color and are found in streams among the decaying leaves, debris or water plants. The larva has a tough skin, but if it is pierced the liquid drains out making an unattractive bait. However, it has a small hard head which it withdraws into its body when disturbed. This head can be pulled out and the hook can be inserted through it. Or you can use thread to tie the larva to the hook. It can be used for trout, bluegills, perch and other pan fish.

When gathering the above insects from any stream or lake, great care should be taken to see that you don't disturb the bottom formation and vegetation too much. When you turn over stones in searching for insects put them back again the way you found them. If you use a screen or net, don't dump the debris that accumulates in it on dry land. Pick out the insects you want to keep and then wash the rest off into the water. In this way you will save hundreds of tiny insects which are hidden among the debris or are too small to be noticeable. If dumped on dry land much of this stream life will perish. Some states have laws regulating the taking of water insects from trout streams. They usually allow an angler to take insects for his own use as bait. The small numbers of insects removed by anglers rarely hurts the trout streams, but if a great many are taken by bait dealers when they gather them to sell, then much harm can be done.

Chapter V

LAND INSECTS

THE INSECTS FOUND ON LAND GREATLY OUTNUMBER THOSE WHICH ARE found in the water, and many of them are eaten by fish if they fall or are blown into the water. Heavy rains and floods also wash land insects into streams, lakes and rivers. Like the water insects, the land insects go through 3 or 4 stages of development from the egg to the adult. There are so many land insects that general methods cannot be laid down for obtaining, keeping and hooking them, and they vary even more than water insects in size, structure and habits. Each insect must be dealt with individually. Although most land insects can be used as bait, only the larger and the most popular ones can be considered here.

GRASSHOPPERS

There are many kinds of grasshoppers found in the fields which can be used as bait. Most of them are the short-horned grasshoppers which are considered locusts and include many species. Those that belong to the genus *Melanoplus* are commonly used, but there are many others which can also be used. It is up to the angler to find out which are most numerous in his locality and which attract the most fish. A few like the big gray-brown or smaller red-brown flying kind are too hard to catch and do not seem to appeal to the fish. Others like the green long-horned grasshoppers and the katydids are somewhat delicate and hard to keep on the hook.

Grasshoppers are most numerous and the largest in the late summer and early fall months. During the daytime when the sun is high they are quite active and hard to catch. But at night or early in the morning when the grass and weeds are damp and the air is cold, they

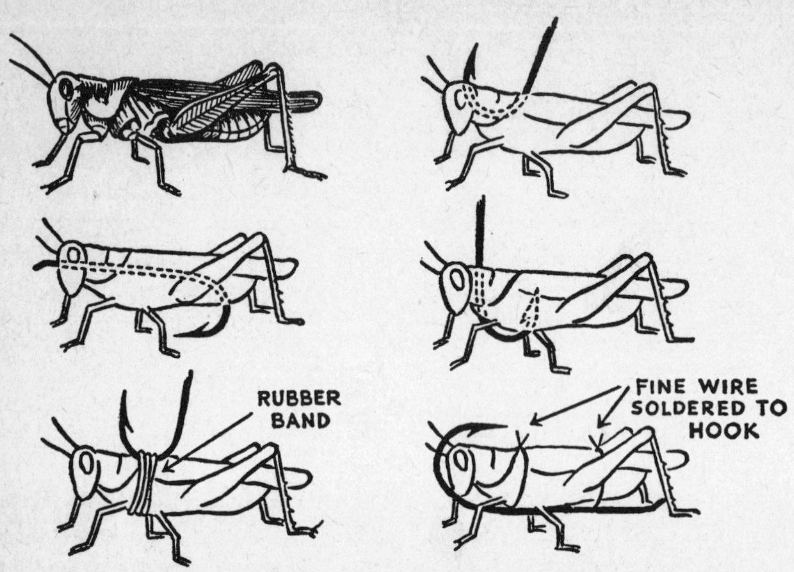

Grasshopper and Methods of Hooking

can be picked up more easily. If you must catch them during the daytime you can use a small butterfly net or fly swatter to pin them down against the grass. They can be kept in a light, cloth bag through which air can enter. Tie the opening with a string and you can allow one grasshopper at a time to emerge when you need it. A cigar box makes a good container for grasshoppers and other land insects. Cut out a small square on the top and cover it with wire screening to allow air to enter. To remove the insects or put them in the box one at a time, a small hole should be bored in the cover of the box and covered with a small sliding door which can be cut out of a sheet of metal. A couple of screws will hold the door in place and keep the hole covered until it is slid open. A handful or two of grass or clover will keep the insects in the box contented and alive during the fishing trip.

There are several ways of hooking the grasshopper. One method is to run the point of the hook into the grasshopper's back about a half-inch from the front of the head and then bring the point of the hook out at the top of the head between the eyes. Another method is to run the point of the hook into the grasshopper's back at the neck and bring it out at the underside and then run it again into the abdomen. Still another way is to run the point into the front of the head between the eyes and push the hook through most of the hopper's body letting it come out near the tail end of the abdomen.

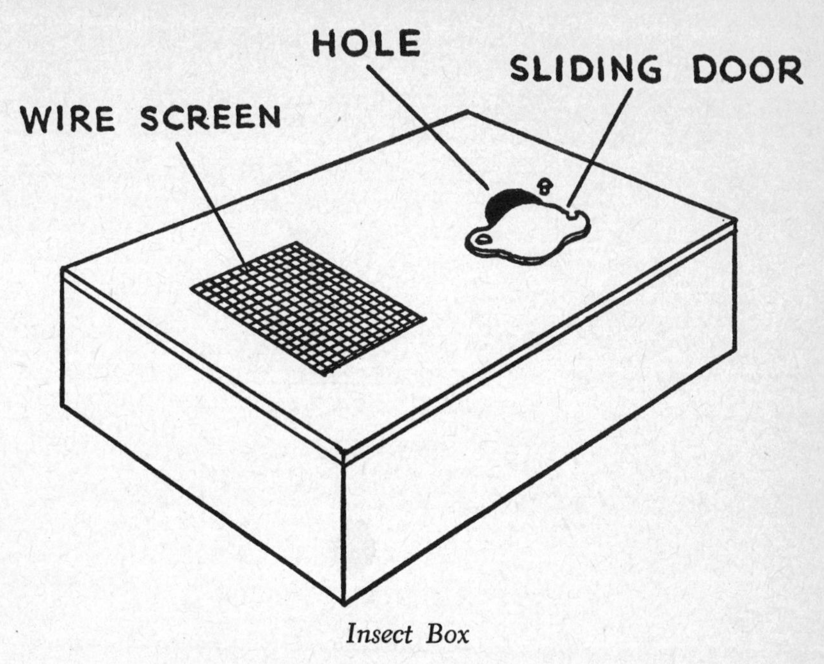

Insect Box

Of course, the above methods tend to kill the grasshopper rather quickly and many anglers prefer other methods. Some solder two pieces of fine wire to the shank of the hook and wrap these around the grasshopper. Others use a thin rubber band and slip several turns around the body of the grasshopper just in front of the two hind legs. Then the hook is run under the rubber bands. Or they tie the grasshopper to the hook with silk or cotton thread. Grasshoppers will take trout, black bass, catfish and pan fish.

CRICKETS

The larger dark-brown or black field crickets which are found in the grassy fields are popular as bait for many fresh-water fishes. There are several species of field crickets but the one usually preferred is the common black field cricket (*Gryllus assimilis*) which is one of the largest. Crickets like grasshoppers are most numerous and the largest in size during the late summer and early fall months. They can be found under stones, hay piles, and wheat, corn or rye stacks. You can also attract crickets by using stale bread as a lure. After they are caught they can be kept in the same types of containers as those used for grasshoppers. If you are keeping them for several days you can feed them grass, moist bread or lettuce.

Cricket and Method of Hooking

But catching crickets in large numbers is quite a chore and many anglers prefer to raise their own. Experiments at the Alabama Polytechnic Institute have shown that the common black field cricket can easily be raised in large numbers. Metal cans such as garbage cans, lard cans, metal drums with tops removed and similar containers are best to use. The can should be kept indoors in a garage, basement, barn, woodshed or empty room. If the building is screened, the top of the can could be left open. But if it is not, a piece of window screen should be used as a cover to keep out spiders, ants and other parasites which may harm the crickets. The container should be sandpapered on the inside for about 8 or 10 inches from the top. Then this area is coated with floor wax and polished to keep the insects from climbing out. From 4 to 6 inches of fine, clean, damp sand is spread on the bottom of the can. It must feel damp to the touch in order for the crickets to lay their eggs in it. To provide cover for the young crickets a layer of 4 or 5 inches of excelsior or straw should be spread over the sand. Then the container should be stocked with an equal number of male and female crickets. The females can be recognized by the long tube protruding at the tail end which is used to deposit eggs. From 20 to 50 crickets may be needed to stock the can depending on its size. Poultry laying mash has proved to be one of the best foods for crickets. A small tray or saucer should be filled with the mash and placed in the container. To supply the crickets with water a small glass jar fountain such as those used by poultrymen is good. The saucer holding the water on the bottom should be filled with cotton to prevent the young crickets from drowning.

The crickets will thrive during the warmer months and produce from 200 to 500 young, depending on the size of the container and your original stock. During the colder months, if you want the crickets to grow and reproduce, suspend an electric light bulb to within 5 or 6 inches of the excelsior in the can. It takes the crickets about 3 months to reach maturity if the heat is maintained at around 80° F. The eggs usually hatch in 15 to 25 days and the young crickets become large enough to use as bait in about a month.

Crickets are rather delicate and are hard to keep on a hook. Small, fine wire hooks should be used and the hook should be run under the collar either with the point towards the head or away from it. They can also be hooked like the grasshopper, running the hook from the back through the neck, then out on the underside and into the abdomen. You can also use the hooks with the wire soldered to the shank or tie the cricket to the hook with cotton or silk thread. Crickets will take trout, black bass, sunfish and other pan fish.

COCKROACHES

Although cockroaches are repulsive to many people, others find that they make good bait for pan fish. They can be found in warehouses, garbage pails and dumps where they are especially active at night. They are fast runners and difficult to catch but can often be captured in good numbers in traps baited with a raw potato, apple or bread soaked in water. They can also be raised in containers similar to those used for crickets. Two species, the German cockroach or Croton bug (*Blattella germanica*) and the American cockroach (*Periplaneta americana*) are best for raising.

The containers used should be covered with cheesecloth or wire screen to prevent the roaches from escaping. Some oil or vaseline smeared near the top of the container will keep them from escaping when it is opened. Roaches will eat many foods such as lettuce, fruits and vegetables. A mixture containing 50 percent whole ground wheat, 45 percent dried skim milk and 5 percent dried baker's yeast is recommended as a stock diet. This mixture is moistened with water, then

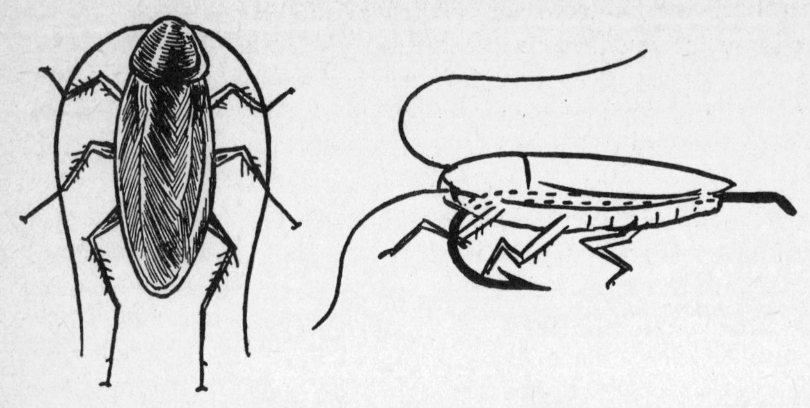

Cockroach and Method of Hooking

allowed to dry. Cockroaches drink plenty of water and this can be furnished in the same type of glass jar fountain as used for crickets.

Roaches are aslo delicate and should be threaded on a hook tail first with the hook running the full length of the body and the point and barb penetrating up to the head. They are used frequently for bluegills and other sunfishes.

MAGGOTS

These larvae of flies are another bait which is repulsive to the average angler. But this may be mainly because they are usually associated with manure, garbage or decaying flesh. If the maggots are properly cleansed they can be handled with little trouble. The best maggots for bait are the larvae of the housefly, the stable fly and the blowfly. The housefly maggot is smaller than the other two and is usually found in garbage. The stable fly maggots are found in manure, while the blowfly maggots live in decaying flesh.

To obtain blowfly maggots you can hang a piece of meat or a small dead animal outdoors to attract the adult flies. They will lay their eggs on the meat and these will hatch into tiny larvae. In about three or four days the maggots will reach their full growth and then you can knock them off with a stick into a container filled with cornmeal or bran. This will scour the maggots and make them dry and more pleasant to handle. Maggots will take whitefish and the various pan fishes.

MEAL WORMS

These yellow and brown larvae of the beetle are considered pests because they spoil grains in mills, grain stores, grain elevators, feed bins and other places where these foods are stored. But meal worms are also used as food for various pets and as bait for pan fish. They can be found where grain is stored or bought from pet shops and aquarium dealers. The meal worm may reach an inch in length and two species, the yellow meal worm (*Tenebrio molitor*) and the dark meal worm (*Tenebrio obscurus*), are commonly found. They can be raised in a large washtub or box with smooth inside walls and a cover of wire screen or cheesecloth to prevent the escape of the larvae and adults. A layer of chicken mash or other grain meals is spread to a depth of ¼ inch on the bottom of the container. Then a layer of burlap is used to cover this food, more mash is sprinkled over the burlap, and this is also covered with a layer of burlap. Several alternate layers of feed and burlap should be built up to provide food and hiding places for the larvae. This box will need a sprinkling of water each day, or some raw carrots or potatoes should be placed in the container to provide the necessary moisture. Then you can stock the container with several hundred meal worms. These will turn into adults which will lay eggs to provide more meal worms and some of the adults can be removed to other boxes to start new cultures.

GRUBS

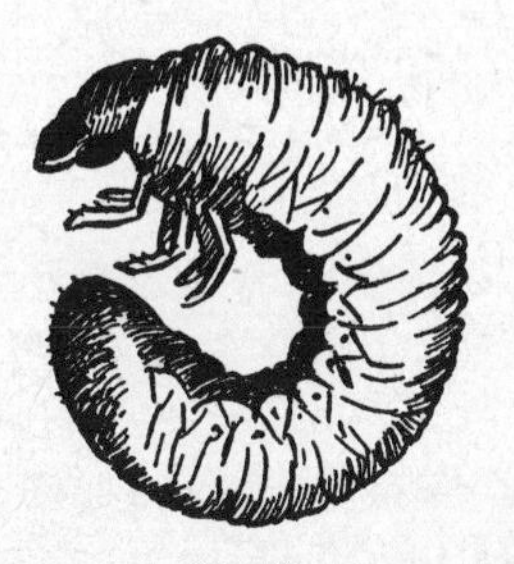

Grub

Although the adult beetles are eaten by fish and can be used for bait, it is the larvae which are more commonly used for this purpose. The big, white grubs of the June bug and the Japanese beetle are found in the ground where they feed on the roots of grasses, shrubs, trees and other plants. There are many kinds of beetles and some of their grubs live in rotting stumps, logs, posts, under the bark of trees and in animal dung. Many of these make good baits for bass, trout and pan fish. They have rather delicate bodies and should be tied on to the hook or impaled through the head. Some of them turn black soon after they are killed and become less effective baits. Grubs can be kept until wanted in the same substances in which they are found.

CATALPA WORM

This caterpillar is the larva of the sphinx or hawk moth. It may reach a length of 3 inches and has a smooth body which is dark brown or black on the back and green along the sides. They are also known as "catawbies" and are found in catalpa trees, which are their only source of food. The trees may produce two or more crops a year from May to September. The worms can be picked off the tree and kept dormant in an icebox or refrigerator for a few weeks until they are ready to be used. Some anglers turn them inside out with a stick or nail before using them as bait. But they can be used as they are, or cut in half for bluegills and other sunfish.

CATERPILLARS

There are many other caterpillars of the butterflies and moths which can be used as bait. Those with short hairs are generally not as good as those with smooth bodies. That great pest the European corn borer, which does so much damage to corn, is a caterpillar which can be used for bait. It can be found on the leaves, under the husks, and in tassels during the summer months. During the late fall and winter they can be found in the dry stalks which remain in the fields. They make good pan fish baits during the summer, and in the winter for fishing through the ice for bluegills. Another caterpillar which attacks corn and also cotton, tomatoes, tobacco and other crops is the corn earworm, which can also be used for bait. The green caterpillars found on cabbage leaves are used by some anglers. Another small green caterpillar is found during the summer months on oak trees. It can be obtained by shaking the branches over a cloth or paper, and will take trout and pan fish.

Caterpillars usually have thin skins and should be hooked through the tougher head or tied on with thread. Hooking them deep through the body will cause the body fluids to seep out and kills them quickly.

The pupae of moths, which are usually enclosed in cocoons, and those of butterflies, which are naked, can also be used as bait. This is the resting stage of the insect in its transformation from the larva or caterpillar to the adult moth or butterfly. Those with cocoons should be removed from the silk covering before using.

GALL WORMS

The larvae found in the galls or swellings on the stems of plants can be used for bait. These are usually the larvae of flies, moths or wasps. A popular bait is the small white larva found in the gall on the stem of the goldenrod plant. These gall worms make good winter bait for bluegills since they can be obtained easily when other baits are scarce. The galls can be collected in the fall or early winter and stored in a cool, dry place until needed. Split open the gall with a knife and your bait is ready for use.

CICADA

The cicadas, harvest flies and seventeen-year locusts are sometimes used as bait for bass, trout and catfish. These are the big insects with transparent wings, blunt heads and large eyes. There are many species and

Cicada

they appear almost every year, but are numerous only during certain years. The males can easily be located when they sing loudly and shrilly while clinging to a tree, post or plant. But to catch them is another matter and you have to sneak up quietly and make a quick grab.

WASPS, BEES AND HORNETS

The adults of these stinging insects can be used as bait but few anglers have the courage to tackle the task of obtaining them and then using them. The small larvae or grubs found in the combs or nests of bees, wasps, hornets and yellow jackets are less of a problem and are sometimes used as bait.

Of course, there are many other land insects which haven't been mentioned here which also make good baits. If you see anything that flies, crawls or hops that looks big enough to tempt a fish, give it a trial and most of the time you will find that the fish will take it. One of the best things about land insect baits is that they are so varied and numerous that there is almost always some kind of bait available. This comes in handy if you run out of bait and would like to continue fishing. A search in the grass, weeds, shrubs, and under stones generally produces some kind of insect which can be used for bait.

Chapter VI

OTHER BAITS

THIS SECTION WILL DEAL WITH THE MISCELLANEOUS BAITS WHICH DO not readily fall into the groups considered so far. The methods used in obtaining, keeping and hooking the baits will be found in the part alloted to each bait.

CRAYFISH

This small crustacean is easily recognized, since it looks like a miniature lobster. It is also called the crawfish, crawdad, craw, and crab. There are some 100 species found in the swamps, brooks, creeks, lakes and rivers of the country. Some grow larger than others but most of them fall between 2 and 5 inches in length. Some prefer the riffles of streams while others are found in the quieter pools and still others in ponds and lakes. Some even live in burrows which they dig in wet fields and hillsides. But most of them, no matter where found, can be used as bait.

Crayfish are more or less scavengers and feed on a wide variety of plant and animal matter. They are active at night, when they leave their hiding places under stones and in burrows to come into shallow water to feed and molt. This molting is necessary because the crayfish has a hard shell which does not allow it to grow until it is cast off to make room for the expanding tissues. Just before the crayfish gets rid of its hard shell it is known as a "peeler." After it casts it off, it becomes a "soft-shell" and when the new shell starts to harden a day or so later it is called a "paper-shell." Then when the new shell hardens completely it becomes a "hard-shell" again. Crayfish make good baits in all their various stages but are best when they are soft-shelled.

Crayfish can be caught by hand, with dip nets or with seines. You can usually find them in the daytime by turning over stones or searching in the weed beds. Sometimes they can be dug out of their burrows in clay or sand banks. But the best time to catch them is at night, using a flashlight and a dip net or seine. Some anglers also use minnow traps or specially constructed wire traps with funnel entrances, baited with dead fish or meat. These can be left overnight and checked in the morning. However, the majority of the crayfish caught by this method will be hard ones.

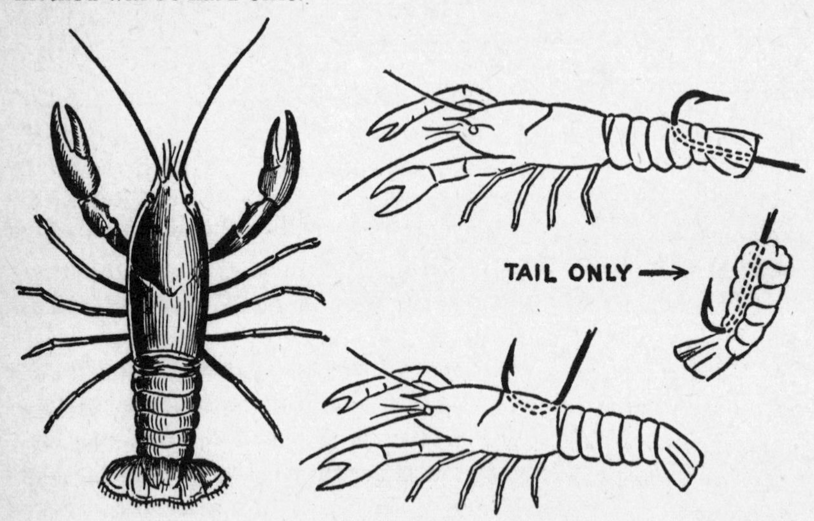

Crayfish and Methods of Hooking

Anglers are always searching for a method which will turn hard-shelled crayfish into soft ones. But the only foolproof method is to let nature take its course and help it along a bit by feeding the crayfish so that they grow as rapidly as possible and molt more often. Crayfish will live in minnow ponds, pools and tanks supplied with running water. Here you can feed them pieces of meat or dead fish and have soft-shelled crayfish on hand when you need them. If you have several ponds or tanks you can be sure that some crayfish will be molting. And since the smaller ones grow faster and shed more often it is best to stock the tanks with small and medium-sized crayfish. Always remove the excess food and dead crayfish from the pools or tanks immediately to prevent contamination. It is also wise to separate the crayfish according to size, since the larger ones will often attack and cripple or kill the smaller ones. The soft-shelled crayfish should also be removed from the tanks as soon as possible to prevent them from being killed or eaten.

If soft-shelled crayfish are to be used soon they can be kept in a container filled with damp moss. But if they are to be kept for several days, they should be placed with the moss in a refrigerator or icebox where they will stay soft for a few days. The cold will help prevent the shells from hardening, but after they are removed from the ice they should be used immediately. Hard-shelled crayfish can be carried in a container filled with damp moss or grass. Here too, always keep the hard-shelled crayfish separated from the soft-shelled ones.

Crayfish are used for many fresh-water fishes such as trout, black bass, walleyes, catfish, carp, suckers and pan fish. They make one of the best baits available for smallmouth bass. The hard-shelled crayfish are generally hooked through the tail, with the point and barb facing either up or down. Some anglers hook them through the back, but since bass and other fish usually swallow the crayfish tail first, the tail method of hooking is better. Some anglers also break off the big pincers to make the bait more attractive and easier to handle. The tails of hard-shelled crayfish make excellent baits, too. These can be broken off and used as is, or peeled and then threaded on the hook.

The soft-shelled crayfish are much harder to keep on the hook and usually have to be lashed on with fine silk or cotton thread, or else rubber bands can be used to hold them on. Or you can solder two pieces of fine wire to the shank of the hook and use these to tie the crayfish down.

FROGS

These amphibians are another bait which is popular with many anglers, especially for large fish. There are many species of frogs, but four kinds are used more than any others. The bullfrog (*Rana catesbiana*) is one of the largest. It is light gray-green and sometimes brown-green in color above, and yellow-white underneath. The bullfrog is usually found in the larger shallow ponds and lakes. It is sought a great deal for food and is scarce in many areas. Only the smaller bullfrogs make practical baits.

Another frog is the green frog (*Rana clamitans*) which is often confused with the bullfrog, but which has a dark, greenish-brown back and a vivid green head and shoulders. The throat is bright yellow and the belly a creamy white. It is found in the same places as the bullfrog and in many other fresh waters.

Green Frog

Leopard Frog

One of the frogs most widely used as bait is the leopard frog (*Rana pipiens*). This frog has a ground color of rich green which is sometimes brownish, and the familiar spots on the back which are more or less rounded and edged with light bands. It lives in the grass along streams, brooks, ponds and springs, but it often travels far inland and is found quite a distance from water at times.

Another frog which is widely used for bait is the pickerel frog (*Rana palustris*), which resembles the leopard frog but is mostly brown in color and has dark yellow or orange on the inside of its hind legs and the lower part of the abdomen. The spots are square instead of round like those on the leopard frog. While it also prefers the shorelines of lakes, brooks, streams and ponds it rarely ventures as far away from water as the leopard frog. There are many other species of frogs in this country which can also be used as bait.

Frogs can be caught by hand if you are fast enough, or with a long-handled dip net. Look for them in the weeds growing in the water and in the grass along the edge of lakes, ponds and streams. The best time to hunt them is at night, when you can use a flashlight to blind them and when they usually remain in one place until disturbed. Some of the larger frogs can even be caught on a hook baited with a worm or piece of red cloth and dangled in front of them.

Frogs can be kept in a live box made of wire mesh partly submerged in the water and filled with some rocks so that they can come up to breathe and rest. They will also live in a container or tank kept in a cool spot and filled with a few inches of water. Some rocks or a board should be placed on the bottom to allow the frogs to leave the water. They will eat worms and insects that are alive and moving, and worms and strips of meat will often be taken if dangled in front of them.

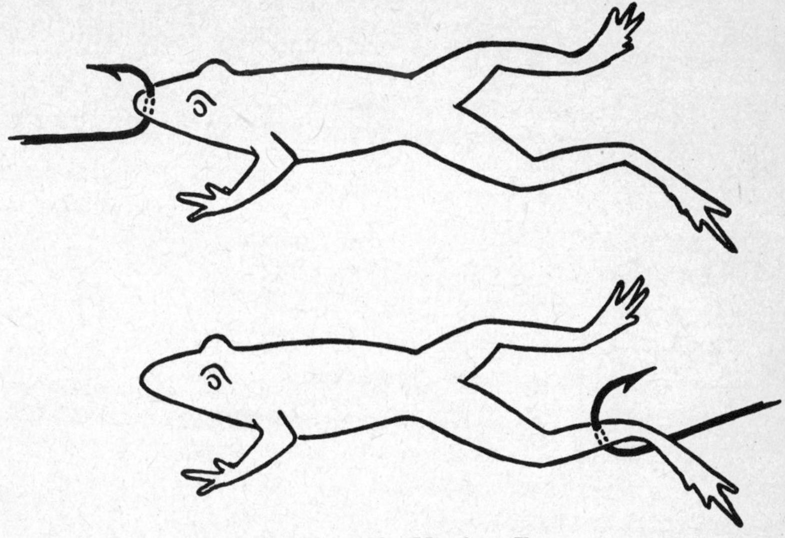

Two Ways To Hook a Frog

The usual method of hooking frogs is through both lips, with the hook entering underneath and coming out on top. They can also be hooked through the front or hind leg. There are many frog harnesses on the market which do not injure the frog, and some even have weed guards so that the angler can fish the frogs in the weeds and lily pads. Whichever method of hooking is used it is important to keep the frog lively and kicking as much as possible. The legs of large frogs can be skinned and used for pickerel if they are skittered through the water to give them action. Tadpoles or the immature frogs can also be used for bait. Frogs will take black bass, pike, pickerel, muskellunge, large trout and catfish. Before catching or using frogs check your fish and game laws, since many states have regulations governing the taking and use of these baits.

TOADS

Small toads also make good baits at times. The trouble is that they are often difficult to obtain in any quantities, but there are times when they are very numerous and swarm all over the woods. They can also be found in gardens at night when they come out to feed. Toads are used for black bass and catfish.

SALAMANDERS AND NEWTS

These lizardlike creatures are amphibians, like frogs, and are sometimes found in the water and sometimes on land. There are many species, some of them reaching a foot in length, but most of them are only a few inches long. They live in brooks, springs, lakes and streams or on land in moist places. They are active at night and during the day hide under logs, stones, in moss, holes and the overhanging banks of streams. Others can be found in the riffles of streams under rocks, logs and other debris. They can be caught by hand or with seines. Grab them near the head or midsection because many salamanders and newts have tails which break off easily. They can be kept for short periods of time in containers filled with damp moss and placed in a cool spot. For longer periods, tanks or aquariums with running water are best. They can be fed insects, meal worms, earthworms and small bits of meat or fish.

Salamander

Salamanders are hooked through one of their legs, or at the base of the tail, or just under the skin. But care must be taken in casting them since they are rather delicate. They will take trout, black bass, catfish and pan fish.

SALMON EGGS

Salmon eggs are a very popular bait for steelhead trout, especially during the winter months when other methods fail to interest the fish. They are also used for other trout where it is legal, but since many states prohibit the use of salmon eggs for game fish it is best to check your local game laws before using this bait.

Salmon eggs are sold in many tackle stores and can be purchased in small jars, but many anglers do not consider the packed eggs as good as those taken from a freshly killed salmon or steelhead trout. Eggs taken from fish which are ready to spawn can be used singly, since they are big. But those from fish in which the eggs are not ripe, are small in size and are usually used in clusters of a dozen or more eggs. The egg sacs taken from the female salmon or steelhead trout can be cut with scissors into "gobs" of any size bait you wish to use. The membrane which is attached to the eggs helps to hold them in place, but they still wash off easily or fall off the hook when cast. Therefore many anglers tie them on the hook with thread, or loop the leader over them, or enclose them in small bags of cheesecloth, mosquito netting or a similar mesh.

Various processes are used by commercial packers to preserve and color their eggs. These they are reluctant to reveal. However, by using the following methods and experimenting a bit you can find the one which gives the best results. If you get from a freshly killed fish some eggs which you plan to use soon, you can merely harden them by sprinkling them lightly with salt or borax; roll them up in paper and place them in a refrigerator or icebox.

To prepare eggs for longer periods of time, get fresh, large, firm eggs which separate readily from the membrane. Then split open the egg sacs and pour hot water over the eggs to separate them from the membrane. The process can be helped along by rubbing the eggs lightly over a wire mesh screen. But don't use so much hot water that it damages the thin membranes enclosing each egg. Now put the eggs in a solution of 1 part sugar to 3 or more parts of salt—as much as 9 parts salt can be used. The brine solution should test 80 to 90 percent by salinometer. Aniline dyes can be added to give the eggs a red coloring. The eggs should then be stirred around in the solution with a wooden paddle from 20 to 30 minutes to cure and color them. Properly cured eggs won't be too hard, brittle, rubbery or shrunken. Finally the eggs are drained and packed in airtight jars. If the jars remain closed the eggs will keep for a long time in a cool place. However, in warm climates a solution of 5 percent formalin can be added. Another preservative which is often added is 1 percent sodium benzoate. The same process can be used to preserve cluster eggs, except that they are merely washed in ordinary cold water before being placed in the brine solution, and they are allowed to cure in the solution somewhat longer than single eggs before being drained and packed in jars.

Another method of preserving salmon eggs is to keep them in a salt solution strong enough to just barely float the eggs until the slime is cut. Then they should be drained, put in glycerin and kept in airtight jars in a cool place. When these eggs are to be used, they should be drained of glycerin and placed in separate tightly covered containers. Once the eggs have been removed from the glycerin they should not be put back in it.

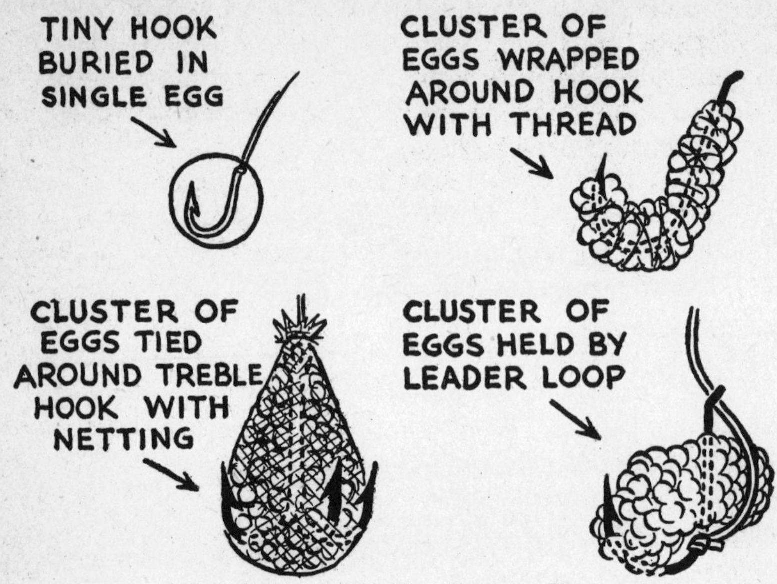

Methods of Hooking Salmon Eggs

There are many methods of hooking salmon eggs, depending on the size of the eggs and the fishing being done. When using large single eggs, small short-shanked hooks from about size No. 10 to 14 are used. The bend and shank of the hook is buried in the egg and often even the eye of the hook is pushed into the egg. Clusters of eggs can be wrapped around the shank and bend of a single hook or treble hook with fine, red-colored silk or cotton thread. Some anglers enclose the cluster around a single or treble hook with a small piece of cloth netting and tie it above the hook to form a small bag. But one of the most popular procedures is to tie up 2 or 3 dozen sacks in advance, using 3-inch squares of cheesecloth or other netting which is usually red in color. The egg cluster is placed in the center of the square and the corners of the netting are gathered in and tied with red thread to form a small sack. Such enclosed clusters of eggs can be placed on a hook by running the point into the sack just below the tie, then burying the bend in the eggs and allowing the point and barb to protrude from the netting. Some anglers don't use any netting, but run their leader through the eye of a hook, then make a sliding tie on the shank forming a loop which tightens around the cluster of eggs.

LEECHES

These are the familiar bloodsuckers which are found in most ponds, streams and lakes. There are many species and they vary in size and color. But they can easily be recognized by their wormlike shapes and the fact that they have sucking discs at each end of their bodies. Not all of them suck blood; some of them feed on tiny animals and plant matter.

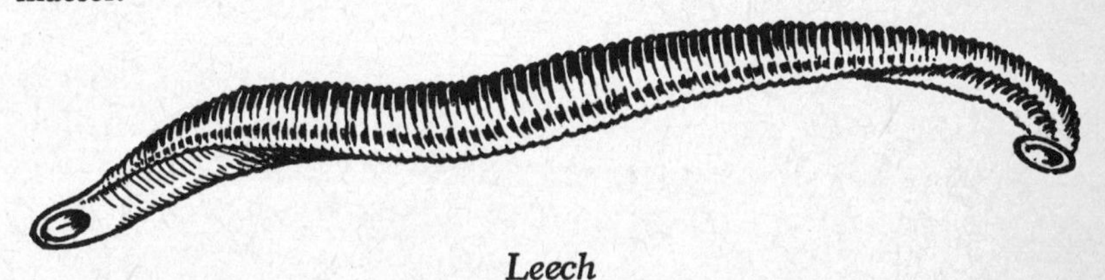

Leech

Leeches can sometimes be caught in traps similar to the minnow type, which are baited with fresh meat or coagulated blood. They can also be caught with a seine or dip net. Leeches usually remain well hidden, but if you stir up the water by wading through it and kicking up the mud and weeds they'll often come out. When they attach themselves to the bare skin they can be removed by pulling hard. These aquatic worms can be kept in an aquarium or other container filled with water. They will live for a long time without food so there is no need to feed them. Leeches will take black bass, trout and catfish when used as bait.

CLAMS AND MUSSELS

There are many species of fresh-water clams and mussels found in the streams and rivers. They lie partly buried in the mud, sand or gravel bottom and can easily be gathered by hand in shallow water. In deeper water you may have to feel them out with your bare feet or dive down and dig them out. To take them in larger quantities, large curved hooks with four prongs are dragged along the bottom to catch between the shells and bring them up. Some states have regulations governing the taking of clams, to be consulted for size limits and seasons.

The clams can be kept in a live box submerged in the water for quite a while, or for short periods in containers filled with water. To open them just hit them hard against a hard object and crack the shells to remove the soft meat. Or you can insert a knife blade between the shells and cut the hinge muscle.

Fresh-Water Mussel

Clams are good bait for catfish, carp, buffalo, suckers, and will also take pan fish at times. Even bass have been caught on them. For catfish the soft meat from the clams is allowed to sour before using. It can be placed in a jar with sour milk and allowed to stand for several days before using.

SNAILS AND SLUGS

Some of the larger land and water snails can be used for bait. The land snails can be found under stones, logs, and in damp places. The hard shell must be cracked, of course, and the soft body removed. The slugs

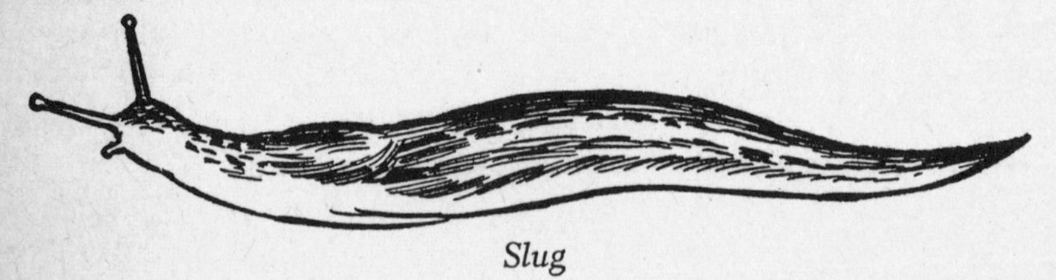

Slug

which are found in gardens, cellars and damp places look like snails without the complete shells and these can also be used for bait. They are used mostly for trout, black bass and pan fish.

SHRIMP

The small salt-water shrimp and prawns are sometimes used for trout and bass. Although these small crustaceans live in salt and brackish water, they can be used in fresh water. They can be caught in salt-water bays along the weedy shores using a fine-mesh seine. They will live best in a wire cage suspended in the water, but they can also be kept in a container lined with cracked ice on the bottom. The ice should be covered with burlap and then the container filled with wood shavings or sawdust and the shrimp placed inside and lightly covered with the shavings or sawdust.

A similar small shrimp is found in fresh water and these are also used at times for bass and pan fish. These small shrimp and prawns aren't very large baits and sometimes 2 or 3 of them on a hook are better than only one.

MICE

Not too many anglers use mice as bait, since they are often hard to obtain and the average angler doesn't care to handle or bait a hook with these rodents. But they sometimes make effective baits for big, wily trout, black bass, pike and muskellunge which do not fall for other baits and lures. The mice used are usually the common house mouse and the field mouse, but there are many other species of small mice which can also be used. Mice can be caught in the regular wire cage traps which take them alive, and these can be bought in almost any hardware store. Field mice can often be caught under stacks of wheat, rye or oats which have been standing for some time. Here you can often find a nest of young mice and these also make good bait, especially for catfish. Mice are usually hooked under the skin or are tied on with wire or thread. Gloves should be used in handling them for they will often try to bite. Mice can easily be raised in quantities in wire cages. Some excelsior for nests, and straw or wood shavings for bedding is needed. The only additional requirements are fresh water to drink and foods like cereals, bread, mash, fruits and vegetables.

SNAKES

Like mice, snakes will never make popular baits due to the average person's dislike for them. But fish like black bass, pike and muskellunge do take them at times. Of course, another reason why they are unpopular is because most people can't tell the difference between the harmless and poisonous species, and therefore avoid them all. This is the safest policy, but if you can recognize the poisonous snakes there is no danger in using the harmless kinds like the ribbon snakes, green or grass snakes, and the smaller garter and water snakes. The green snake rarely bites, but the garter and water snakes will often attempt to bite, so grab them behind the head. Snakes will live for quite a while in almost any container. They'll eat insects, frogs, toads, earthworms or small fish, depending on the species. Snakes can be hooked under the skin or near the base of the tail, near no vital parts.

Chapter VII

PREPARED BAITS

THIS PART DEALS WITH THE VARIOUS FORMULA AND RECIPE BAITS, but it also includes some baits which have not been mentioned so far and which do not readily fall into the previous sections.

DOUGHBALLS

This bait is used mainly for carp, but will also take the buffalo fish and catfishes. There are hundreds of formulas used in preparing it, depending on the individual angler's beliefs and preferences. The basic ingredients are flour, cornmeal, water and some kind of sweetening or flavoring. Some of the more commonly used formulas are listed below and the angler can experiment to find out which one gives the best results in his local waters.

The first recipe will provide one or two anglers with enough bait for a whole day's fishing under normal conditions. Pour 1 cup of water into a pan, add 2 teaspoonfuls of sugar and bring the water to a boil. Then add 1 cup of cornmeal and about ¾ of a cup plain flour to the water. Stir this mixture over a low flame for about 5 minutes. Then place a cover on the pan and put it in a larger pan filled with water (or use a double boiler). The mixture should be cooked for about half an hour. Then stir the mixture once more to test its consistency. If it's too thick you can add a little water, and if too thin you can knead more flour into it. Finally roll the whole thing into a large ball and when it cools it is ready for use. Just pinch off as much as you need to make the doughball.

Another recipe uses ½ cup of plain flour and ½ cup of cornmeal, a pinch of salt, and enough water to form a smooth dough. Mix these ingredients thoroughly and then drop the dough into boiling water and keep it there for about 20 minutes. Then take it out, let it cool and it is ready to use.

Another recipe calls for 1 cup of cornmeal, ½ cup of plain flour and 2 teaspoonfuls of sugar. Add water and mix this into a dough. Form the dough into balls somewhat smaller than you use for bait, since they will become larger after they are cooked, and drop the doughballs into a kettle of boiling water. Keep them there for about 15 or 20 minutes until they are firm and rubbery, and then drain off the water. When it cools the bait is ready for use.

Another recipe calls for 1 cup of plain flour and 2 cups of wheat bran with water added to form a stiff dough. After kneading it thoroughly roll the dough into small balls and cook them in boiling water for 15 or 20 minutes. Then drain off the water and the bait is ready for use when it cools.

Still another recipe requires 2 large potatoes which are peeled and grated, ½ teaspoonful of salt, 1 tablespoon of cornmeal and enough plain flour to make a stiff batter. Then roll into balls of the size desired and drop them into boiling water to cook until they float.

The carp is supposed to have a sweet tooth and many anglers also add either honey, sugar, molasses or corn syrup when making their doughballs.

Absorbent cotton, cornstarch or white of egg are often added to the doughball recipes to help hold the bait together on the hook. But if the doughballs are properly prepared these aids are not needed. In fact, the best doughball bait clings to the hook well, but is still soft enough to mold easily. Doughball bait will keep better on a fishing trip if it is wrapped in wax paper. To keep it longer, wrap it in wax paper and put it in a refrigerator.

The size of the doughball formed around a hook depends on the size of the fish present and the way they are biting. With small fish around, or on days when large fish prefer small baits, only a pinch of dough is molded around the point and barb of the hook. If the fish are large and biting strongly the dough can cover the point, barb and bend of the hook to about halfway up the shank. When the fish are very

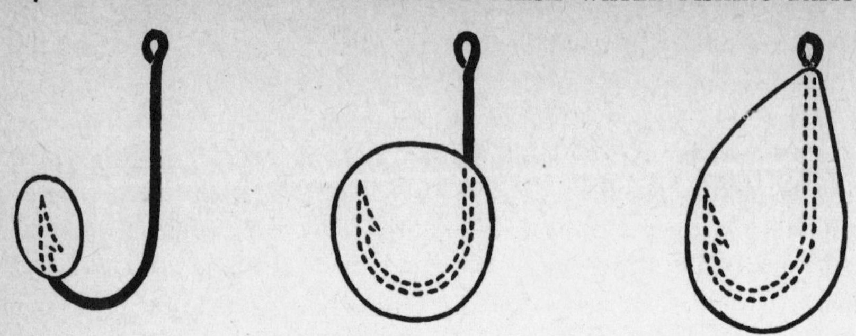

Ways of Baiting Hook With Doughball Bait

large, when fishing in a current or when leaving the bait overnight or for several hours in the water, the whole hook can be covered up to the eye, forming a pear-shaped doughball.

OTHER CARP BAITS

Bread will make a good carp bait at times. Remove the crust and soak the bread in water. Then squeeze out the excess water and knead the bread until it is the right consistency. Whole grains like wheat, rye, barley soaked until they soften are also good. Vegetables like potatoes, carrots and parsnips can be boiled until half done and used as bait. About 4 or 5 kernels of fresh-cut sweet corn can also be used, and canned corn and canned peas. Dried green peas and lima beans can be soaked, parboiled and used as bait. Some anglers even swear by small pieces of marshmallow, or ordinary moss found in the water, rolled into a ball and placed on a hook.

CHEESE AND STINK BAITS

These baits have a strong odor which is supposed to be irresistible to catfish and to attract them from a distance to the hook. Like the doughball bait there are many recipes and formulas for these baits.

One recipe calls for equal parts of Limburger cheese and hamburger meat. A little hot water is added and mixed in well. Now work in enough plain flour to make the bait stick well, and the bait is ready for use. Almost any ground meat or fish can be used with the Limburger cheese and it doesn't have to be fresh. In fact, the riper the meat and the more rancid the cheese, the better the bait.

Another formula uses ½ pound of strong cheese grated fine and mixed with about a quart of plain flour. Water is added to make a stiff dough. Form doughballs of the size desired and let them stand and dry out for a couple of hours, then drop them in boiling water and let them cook for 20 or 30 minutes. Take them out, let them dry again for a while and they are ready to use.

Minnows, pieces of fish or chunks of meat can be placed in a jar and allowed to stand in the sun for a few days. When this bait becomes really "ripe" it is ready to use. The same thing can be done with fresh water mussels or clams, and here many catfishermen add sour milk.

Another stink bait calls for placing minnows or other small fish in a large jar or can and then allowing them to decompose until only an oily substance remains. Small pieces of sponge are soaked in this mess until they absorb the odor, and the sponge is placed on a hook. After using these sponge baits for a while they may lose some of the strong odor and should be removed from the hook and put back into the container to absorb more of the stink.

Another method calls for making the same smelly solution as above and then mixing it with flour to make a stiff dough. You can mold the bait around the hook in any size you want.

Various scents are often added to the stink and cheese baits. Oil of rhodium, oil of anise, asafetida and rotten eggs have all been used. For those anglers who don't like to bother making stink and cheese baits there are quite a few preparations on the market which can be bought already prepared in tackle stores. There are also scents which come in tubes or bottles and which can be spread on baits to lure catfish and other bottom fish.

BLOOD BAITS

Chicken blood which has congealed is a good bait for catfish. This blood can usually be obtained from a poultry market where the chickens are killed. The usual procedure in preparing chicken blood for bait is to obtain a bucket of fresh blood and pour it into a tightly woven cloth bag. This is allowed to hang for a few hours so that the plasma (the colorless liquid) will drain off. The blood left inside will thicken and can be cut up into chunks or strips of the size desired for bait. This bait can be kept for a week or two if placed in a jar and then put in a refrigerator.

To make a tougher chicken blood bait, pour the fresh blood onto a layer of chicken feathers or cotton. After the blood congeals hangs it up to drain and when it hardens you can cut it up into strips with shears.

Other anglers add a couple of tablespoons of powdered waterproof glue to a jar of warm chicken blood to toughen it. The mixture is stirred thoroughly to dissolve the glue, after which the blood is poured into a pan to cool and harden. Still other anglers use alum to toughen the blood.

Plain chicken blood will stay on a hook for a while and a treble hook will hold it better than a single hook. You can also use a short piece of string which can be tied to the line just above the hook. Wrap the string several times around the chicken blood and tuck the end under the barb of a hook. Strips of the tougher chicken blood will stay on a single hook if you run the hook through the strip a few times.

The congealed blood from other poultry, such as turkeys, ducks and geese, can also be used for bait, as well as the blood from cattle, pigs and other animals.

MEAT BAITS

Fresh or decayed meats from various animals make good catfish baits. Beef and pork are usually used. And beef, pork, rabbit, lamb and chicken livers are also effective. These meat baits can be cut into thin strips or chunks and will stay on the hook quite well. Chicken entrails are commonly used for catfish. Many of the above baits will also take eels, especially when used at night.

OTHER CATFISH BAITS

There are few baits which the catfishes won't take at some time or another. Almost all the baits of any size dealt with in this book are eaten by catfish. Many of the larger fishes such as carp, eels and the various pan fishes can be cut up and used for bait. Small animals like mice, rabbits, birds and chicks can all be used. The larger of these can be cut up, while the smaller ones can be used whole. Sometimes catfish will also take berries and fruits. Even small chunks of white laundry soap have caught them. Most expert catfishermen take a wide variety of baits with them and try them all to find out which ones are being taken most readily.

PORK RIND AND PORK CHUNK

Although these baits are usually used like artificial lures or together with artificial lures, they are really a natural bait, being obtained from an animal. And since many anglers would like to know how to prepare and preserve these baits, they will be included here to complete the list. The tough pork rind can usually be obtained from a butcher who sells salt pork if you ask him to save it for you. A very sharp knife or razor blade will cut the rind into strips of any size or shape you desire. Before you do this, though, make sure that all the excess fat has

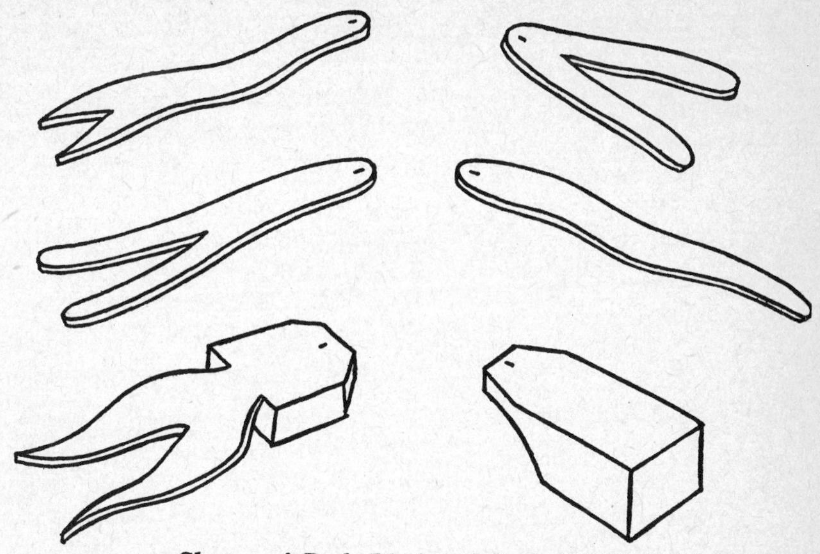

Shapes of Pork Rind and Pork Chunks

been scraped off the rind. Then put your strips in a brine solution strong enough to float a potato. Keep them there for about 2 or 3 days, then remove and bleach them by soaking them in a dilute hydrochloric or acetic acid solution until they turn white. Finally, pack the strips in airtight jars containing a little glycerin and a solution of 10 to 20 percent formalin. A solution of 1 percent sodium benzoate in water can be used instead of the formalin. You can also use ordinary rubbing alcohol or even a heavy brine solution to preserve the pork rind. Some of these solutions are good only for short periods of time, while others preserve the pork rind indefinitely; some stiffen the rind, while others keep it soft. A little experimenting will tell you which one is best suited for your purpose.

Pork chunks are also made from salt pork, but here the rind and an inch or so thickness of the fat is also utilized. If you keep the pork for several days in a solution of formalin, you will find that it toughens the pork and makes it easier to cut.

Of course pork rind strips and chunks already prepared can be bought in almost any tackle store. But most anglers have their own ideas about the best size, shape and weight of pork rind or chunks and prefer to cut and preserve their own.

Chapter VIII

RAISING BAIT FOR PROFIT

At one time, not too long ago, all the live baits used for fishing were obtained as needed by anglers and bait dealers. But with the increased demand for such baits more and more people are starting to raise baits to sell. Some baits have become scarce in many areas because of the increasing demand, and bait dealers find that they can no longer obtain enough to satisfy this need. This shortage of baits has caused many states to pass laws regulating the taking of bait, thus making it still more difficult for the bait dealer to obtain a supply for his customers. Another reason for raising your own bait is that you always have a supply on hand during the seasons when baits are scarce or difficult to obtain.

Many fishing-tackle dealers and those who rent out boats find that it pays to carry a variety of baits in order to attract more customers. Anglers will patronize the boat livery or tackle store which can also sell them live bait when they need it. Since such tackle stores and boat liveries cannot always depend on bait dealers for bait, they find it pays to raise their own if they have the space and facilities.

Many people, too, are discovering that the live-bait business can be highly profitable. Although more and more bait dealers are springing up all over the country, there is plenty of room for others either as full-time bait businesses or part-time suppliers and retailers. During the fishing season in many areas the demand for bait is so great that the dealer can sell out his supply in a short time, and the demand for live baits is bound to increase instead of decrease, since more and more people are taking up fishing. Then too, people are moving from the country to the cities, where they cannot obtain their own bait and must depend on the bait dealers.

Most important of all, however, is that the bait business usually requires a smaller investment of money or material than many other ventures. But, like most businesses, it requires knowledge—of the baits to be raised, methods of handling and distribution. And, of course, some work. However, one advantage is that you can always start off on a small-scale or part-time basis and find out if it is profitable in your area and whether you like the work or not.

No doubt the easiest bait to raise, and one which requires the least investment of time and money, is the earthworm. They can be raised indoors or outdoors. Earthworms are very prolific and by starting off with a few hundred worms you will have thousands in a matter of months and then millions, depending on how big a business you want and the time and space you can devote to it.

There are many so called worm ranches, farms or hatcheries in various parts of the country where you can buy a breeding stock of prolific and lively worms to start your own business. These worm farms have been raising worms for years and have experimented with methods and species of worms to find those which are the most prolific and make the best fish bait. Many of these worm farms provide free literature with each purchase of worms, or sell booklets which will tell you all you need to know to raise worms in large numbers. Look in the classified advertising sections of outdoor magazines like *Field & Stream*, *Outdoor Life* or *Hunting & Fishing* for their addresses.

After you have started raising worms in quantities you will want to sell them. If you live in a locality with good fishing waters near by you can often sell your worms profitably by selling direct to anglers. A sign or two in front of your place or along a well-traveled road is usually all you need. Or if you are some distance from the fishing waters or highways you can sell your worms to tackle stores, boat liveries or bait suppliers. Or advertise in outdoor magazines and sell your worms by mail to anglers and to others interested in starting their own businesses. And don't forget nurseries, farmers and gardeners who want to improve their soil.

Raising minnows for bait is usually a more expensive proposition than raising worms. But the demand for minnows is great and most minnow hatcheries have no trouble selling their stock. More and more states are regulating commercial netting of minnows, so that fewer and fewer bait dealers are depending on minnows seined from public waters. Many of them now raise their own minnows or depend on hatcheries to supply them.

Minnows can be raised fairly cheaply if you have a natural pond which is suitable for their propagation. Otherwise you will have to invest quite a bit of money to construct the necessary ponds and obtain the equipment needed for large-scale operation. Raising minnows in large numbers successfully requires a knowledge of the best species, the construction or selection of the right ponds, the proper breeding, feeding, control of diseases, handling and transportation and other vital information. For those who want to raise minnows in large numbers there is an excellent booklet put out by the U. S. Fish and Wildlife Service called *Propagation of Minnows and Other Bait Species,* which contains plenty of information and can be purchased from the Superintendent of Documents, Washington 25, D. C. for 35 cents. A list of dealers in bait minnows from whom you can obtain a brood stock can be had free from the U. S. Fish and Wildlife Service, Department of the Interior, Washington 25, D. C.

Frogs are popular baits in many localities, but they are difficult to raise artificially and most of those sold are caught in either wild or private ponds. These ponds can be improved to allow a greater number of frogs to breed, live and reach adult size. This usually consists of making an irregular shore line or constructing islands and encouraging plants and attracting insects for the frogs to eat.

Crayfish can be propagated in ponds similar to those used for minnows. They can often be raised together with minnows in the same pond. If the pond is a large one or consists of several small ponds you can raise large numbers of crayfish and have plenty of bait for sale. And with large numbers of crayfish present you can also have a good supply of soft-shelled crayfish on hand, because some of them will always be shedding during the summer months. These bring good prices and attract customers who will also buy other baits you may carry.

The water insects such as nymphs and hellgrammites are difficult or impractical to raise artificially and you will have to obtain your own bait from streams and lakes or buy them from bait dealers.

Some of the land insects like crickets and cockroaches are easily raised in large numbers. Meal worms can be raised for fishing and can also be sold to pet shops and aquarium dealers. Then there are the various prepared baits for catfish, carp and other fish which can be made up and packed in cans or jars and sold retail or to bait dealers or through the mail. In recent years more and more of these packaged baits have appeared on the market. In fact most of the natural baits can be preserved and sold in package form to tackle stores or through the mail. And while the preserved baits are usually not as effective as fresh live baits, they find a ready market among anglers who use them because they are always available and serve in an emergency.

But before you start raising or selling live baits, check your state fish and game department for laws on the subject. Many states regulate the taking, selling and distribution of natural baits when done on a commercial scale. Some states also require special permits and licenses which must be obtained before you can catch or raise bait for sale.

PART TWO

NATURAL
Salt Water
FISHING BAITS

Chapter I

SEA WORMS

THE SEA WORMS HEAD THE LIST AS THE MOST POPULAR BAITS USED IN SALT-water fishing especially along the North Atlantic Coast where many millions are used yearly. Although the sea worms are dug commercially at scattered points along the coast, most of them come from the state of Maine. Sea worms dug in Maine are shipped to many points along the Atlantic Coast and are even flown by plane to the Pacific Coast.

One of the reasons for the popularity of sea worms as bait is that almost all tackle stores and bait dealers along the seacoast carry them throughout the fishing season. Sea worms also stay alive quite a while and are handy to keep and carry. But no doubt the main reason why sea worms are a favorite bait with anglers is that most salt-water fishes will take them.

There are many kinds of sea worms which can be used for bait, but since some kinds are scarce or too small to make practical baits, the field narrows down to the sea worms which are dug commercially and show up most often in tackle stores and bait dealers. Other kinds rarely appear in tackle stores but are numerous enough in certain localities to be obtained by anglers and used for bait. Those which the average salt-water angler is apt to encounter will be dealt with here.

CLAM WORMS

The group of sea worms most numerous in numbers and species are the clam worms which belong to the genus *Nereis*. They are also called sand worms and muck worms along the Atlantic Coast and mussel worms, pile worms and rock worms along the Pacific Coast, depending on the species and where it is found. Numerous species are found in many parts of the world but only a few are important as bait to the salt-water angler. The clam worm can be easily recognized by the body which is rounded on top and flat below. There are distinct segments along their dark, iridescent backs which vary in color from a reddish brown to green and blue. Their undersides are lighter in color and may be pink, orange or red. Along the sides they have two rows of orange or red appendages or "legs" which are used in breathing and swimming.

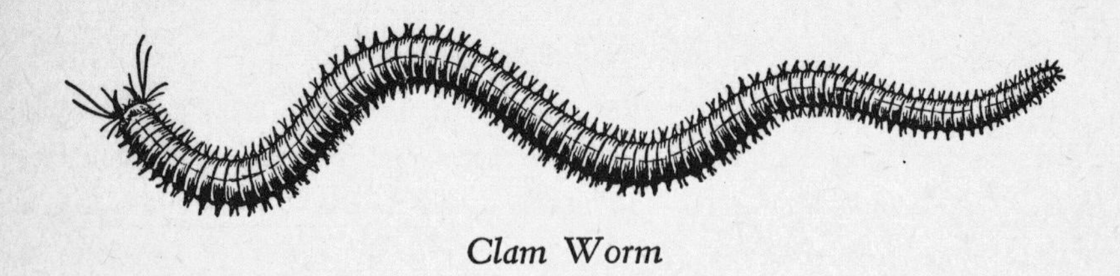

Clam Worm

One of the most common species of clam worm is *Nereis virens,* which is also one of the largest, sometimes reaching 18 inches or more in length. It averages between 5 and 10 inches. It is found from New York northward as far as Labrador along the Atlantic Coast. This popular bait worm prefers muddy and shelly sand where it lives in burrows. It also lives under rocks between low- and high-water marks. At night it often emerges from its burrow and can be found lying on the flats or swimming in shallow water. It has black jaws which it uses in capturing other worms on which it feeds. This is the worm which is usually sold for bait under the name of "sand worm." It is also found along the Pacific Coast but is not as numerous as along the Atlantic Coast.

Another worm closely related to the one above is *Nereis limbata* also called the sand worm. It resembles *Nereis virens* except that it rarely reaches more than 6 inches in length and has light yellow jaws instead of black. It also prefers sandier soil than the other sea worms. This worm is found from Maine to South Carolina.

Another similar worm which is sometimes used for bait is *Nereis pelagica* also called the muck worm, which is smaller than the first two mentioned. The female rarely reaches more than 5 inches, while the males are only 2 inches long. It is reddish-brown in color and the body is widest in the middle. It prefers hard bottoms and is found under stones, among mussels and on shelly bottoms. It is found along the Atlantic Coast from Virginia to Greenland, but is most numerous north of Cape Cod.

The most common species of clam worm found along the Pacific Coast is *Nereis vexillosa* also known as the mussel worm and pile worm. It may reach 12 inches in length but most of those found run from 3 to 6 inches in length. This popular bait is widely distributed along the Pacific Coast from Alaska to San Diego. It lives among mussels, barnacles, rocks, gravel beaches and wharf piles.

The giant clam worm of the Pacific is *Nereis brandti,* which may reach 3 feet or more in length but is not as plentiful as the one above. It is found in sandy mud and under mussel beds from Puget Sound to San Pedro.

BLOOD WORMS

Next to the clam worm in popularity is the blood worm, also called white worm, beak thrower, four-jawed worm and proboscis worm. Other marine worms are often called blood worms but the name is usually associated with the worms belonging to the genus *Glycera.* This worm is easily recognized by its smooth, round body with many narrow, faintly visible segments tapering at both ends. When disturbed it shoots out a long proboscis equipped with four tiny black jaws on the end. In color blood worms vary from light pink to red, often with a purplish tinge. Several species are found in the mud flats along the Atlantic and Pacific Coasts. Some may reach a foot or more in length, but most blood worms average from 6 to 8 inches.

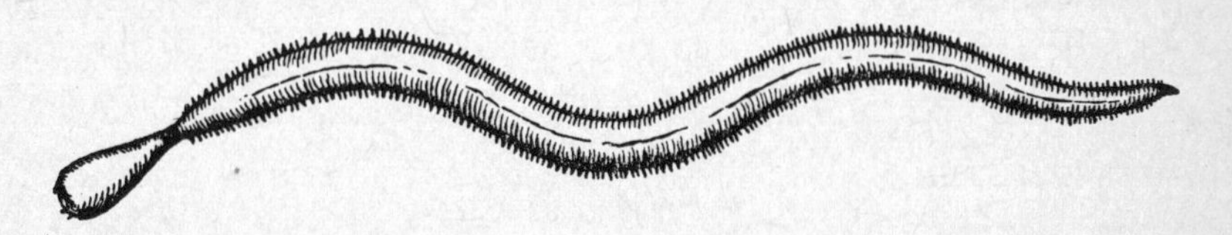

The two kinds of blood worms usually found along the Atlantic Coast are *Glycera dibranchiata* and *Glycera americana.* They are found from the Carolinas to the Bay of Fundy. On the Pacific Coast the two species usually encountered are *Glycera rugosa* and *Glycera robusta.* But they are not too plentiful and blood worms from the Atlantic Coast have been flown to the West Coast to supply the demand of salt-water anglers.

RIBBON WORMS

Another worm sometimes used for bait is the ribbon worm, also called the proboscis worm and tape worm. However, it should not be confused with the tape worms, which are parasites often found in man and animals. The ribbon worm is a marine worm which lives in the sand and mud near low-water mark. The ribbon worm can easily be recognized by its long, flat body which in some species may extend several yards in length. When disturbed it shoots out a long proboscis which is used in burrowing and capturing its prey. There are many species of varying lengths, colors and widths, but those which belong to the genus *Cerebratulus* are mostly used for bait. The ribbon worm *Cerebratulus lacteus,* which is yellowish-white

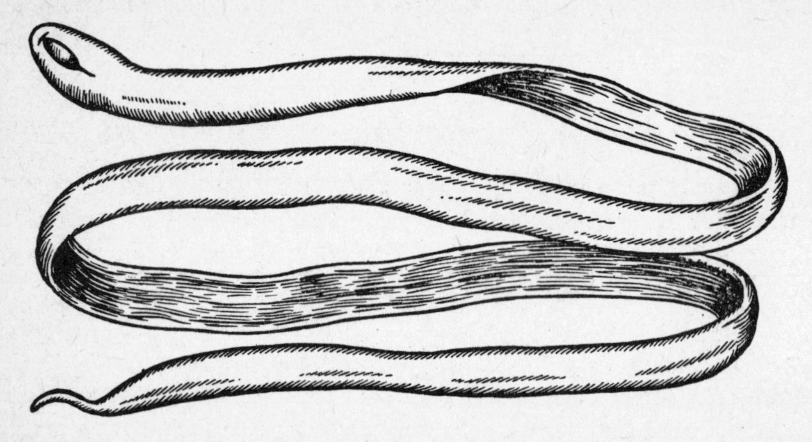

or flesh-colored, is commonly found along the Atlantic Coast from Maine to Florida. Fully grown and stretched out it may reach 20 feet in length and a width of an inch, but most of those found are under 4 or 5 feet. Related species are also found along the Pacific Coast. Ribbon worms are very fragile and should be handled carefully. Even then you'll find that they often break up into small sections.

LUG WORMS

This ugly worm is also used for bait and is also called the burrowing worm. It is found living in sand or mud flats where it has a U-shaped burrow with two openings to the surface. These can be located by looking for the pile of castings around the mouths of the burrows. At low tide the lug worms sometimes emerge and crawl around along the surface. Lug worms have black, brownish or olive-colored skins which are rough and covered with tufts of hairlike gills. The head part is larger than the rest of the body and is filled with a yellowish liquid making it a messy bait. Lug worms may reach a foot in length but most of them run from 4 to 8 inches. The species most commonly obtained along the Atlantic Coast is *Arenicola marina* which is found from Rhode Island southward. On the Pacific Coast *Arenicola claparedii* is the one usually encountered.

Of course, there are many other kinds of sea worms which can be used as bait. Any good-sized worm which you find can be tried and chances are that it will catch fish. Even the earthworms found on land are sometimes

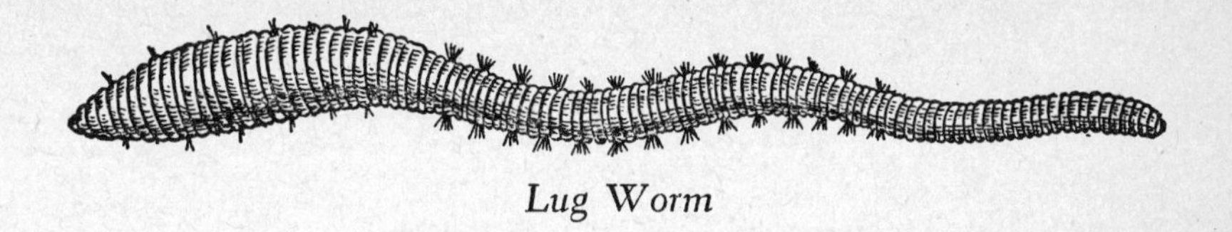

Lug Worm

used to catch flounders, eels, white perch and other fish which are often found in brackish water. They can also be used behind a spinner to catch striped bass if no other worms are available.

OBTAINING, KEEPING AND HOOKING

Most salt-water anglers buy their sea worms from tackle stores, bait dealers or boat liveries, since they do not have the knowledge, equipment, time or energy to dig their own worms. And time and energy are two requisites when digging sea worms, for often it requires a few hours of back-breaking work to dig enough worms for a day's fishing. But in some areas and during certain years the worms are plentiful and can be obtained fairly quickly. Then again, when plenty of worms are needed, you can save some money by digging your own.

The equipment needed to dig sea worms is simple and inexpensive. A pair of boots, a garden fork or clam hoe and a box or pail to keep the worms in will put you in business. During the summer months boots are not essential and an old pair of sneakers can be used, if you don't mind getting your legs covered with mud.

Learning to locate the best places to dig for sea worms will take a little time and experience. Of course, the best way is to find out where other worm diggers gather and go there too. But you can often locate your own mud flats where the worms are present. Clam worms and blood worms prefer a mixture of shelly sand and soft mud where they can be found living in burrows. Sometimes the entrances to these burrows can be noticed. The worms may be anywhere between low- and high-water marks. A good time to dig sea worms is when the tide is about half out to when it is half in again. The most favorable tides usually occur during full moon and new moon since they are extra low and expose a larger area. Try different spots on the mud flats until you locate a colony of worms. Then stay there and dig systematically until the whole section is turned over.

Clam worms and blood worms occur in the same areas but the blood worms will be a few inches under the surface, while the clam worms may be a foot or more beneath the surface. This means that you will usually have to dig at least twice in the same spot to reach the clam worms.

Clam worms can also be obtained on dark nights when they emerge from their burrows and lie exposed on the mud flats. For this you will need a flashlight or better yet, a headlight to spot the worms. They are sensitive to vibrations and strong lights so you have to walk softly and grab them quickly. They can also be captured at times in shallow water with a small dip net.

Other kinds of sea worms can be found among seaweeds, under stones, among mussels and barnacles. The ribbon worms or tape worms are often found in the same areas with clam worms or blood worms, especially where soft clams are plentiful. Lug worms prefer sand or a mixture of sand and mud and the best place to dig is where there are burrow openings with castings around them.

Sea worms are usually easier to obtain during the spring and fall months when the weather is cool. During the summer months they burrow deep to escape the heat. They do the same thing when there is too much rain for they dislike fresh water.

One word of caution about digging sea worms. Some states and towns along our coasts have laws and regulations regarding the digging of sea worms. Some of these require that you be a resident of the state or area or that you need a permit to do such digging. Find out what the laws are in your area before you attempt to dig sea worms.

Although most sea worms are rather delicate and die quickly, they will live for several days and even up to two weeks if properly cared for. Sea worms cannot tolerate too much heat, dryness or fresh water. For best results they should be kept in rockweed, sea moss or sea lettuce which is moist, but not too wet. The worms should be kept in a cellar or other cool spot. An icebox where the temperature is around 40° is a good place to keep worms for several days. The worms should not be allowed to bunch up, and most dealers who handle large quantities of worms have trays which can be turned over each day to keep the worms separated. If the rockweed dries out it can be wetted down with salt water until it is moist. But fresh water should never be used since it can kill the worms. Likewise, worms of each species should be kept in separate containers. Blood worms and clam worms are deadly enemies and often attack one another. And finally all dead sea worms should be removed from the containers as soon as possible.

On a fishing trip most salt-water anglers keep their worms in the small paper boxes in which they are sold. The worms usually stay alive for a day or so in such boxes. But if you have a lot of worms and expect to keep them for more than a day a large wooden box or tray with plenty of moist rock-weed is better. The containers should always be kept out of the sun and in the coolest spot that can be found.

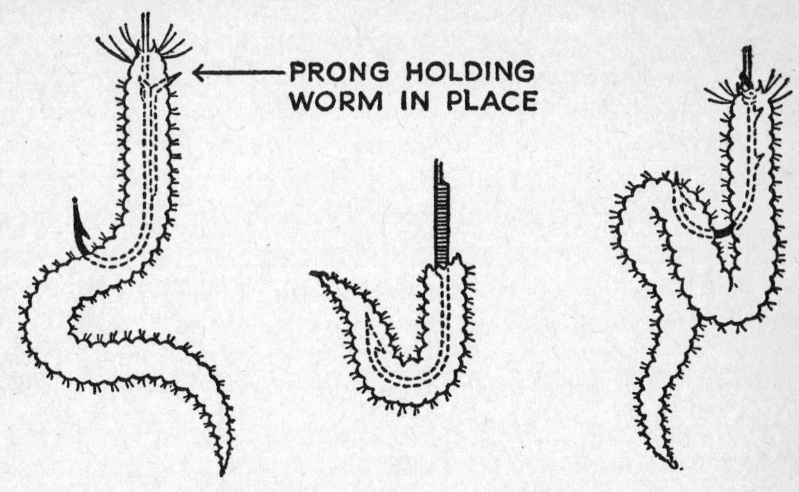

Methods of Hooking Sea Worms

Many anglers would like to know if sea worms can be propagated or raised like earthworms so that they reproduce and can be available in large numbers. Unfortunately, it is difficult or impractical to provide the type of conditions and food the sea worms require to live and reproduce in captivity. So the sea worms must be obtained from the tidewater flats where they are found naturally.

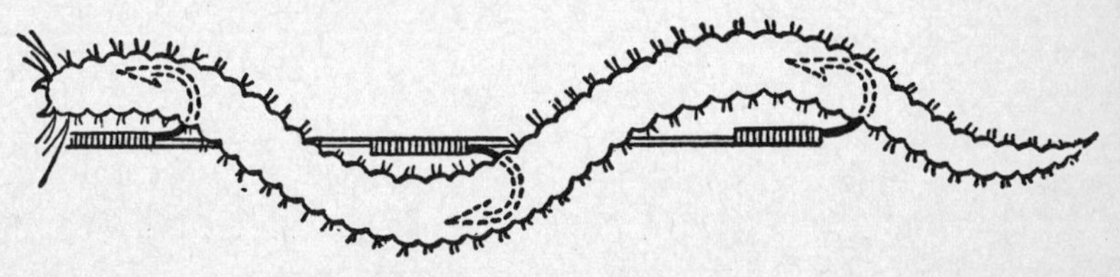

Sea Worm on Gang Hook

There are many methods used in hooking the sea worms, depending on the kind of worm you are using, the type of hooks or rigs and the fish you are seeking. The clam worms or sand worms which are used whole for fairly large fish can be hooked in back of the head, then threaded along the shank until almost half of the worm covers most of the hook, leaving the point and barb exposed. Hooks with sliced shanks are often used to keep the worm from sliding down the hook. Some anglers also wrap a wire prong to the hook shank which extends out at an angle, and when the worm's head is impaled on the prong it is held in place. If the fish are nipping off the tail end of the worm without getting hooked the worm can be looped and hooked through the tail once or twice. Or you can use a gang hook which holds the worm in two or three places. These gang hooks are also used when the sea worms are used in trolling behind spinners. Sometimes two or three sea worms on a hook bring more strikes, especially when the fish are large. For small fish with small mouths pieces of worm from 1 to 3 inches in length are usually best. Almost any fish found in salt water will take clam worms. They are often used for striped bass, tautog or blackfish, scup or porgies, weakfish, flounders, eels, croakers, corbina and other fish.

Hooking Several Sea Worms

Blood worms can be hooked by many of the methods used for clam worms but they have one disadvantage. They do not live long or look attractive if they are cut up into sections. The blood and other liquids ooze out and leave just the skin if the worm is cut. For best results the worm should be placed on the hook whole. When used for striped bass several blood worms on a hook are much better than just one. Blood worms like clam worms are good for most salt-water fishes but are generally preferred for striped bass, flounders, weakfish, northern and southern whiting (also called kingfish), porgies or scup, and tautog or blackfish.

When using sea worms the thing to remember is that when the worms die on the hook and lose their colors, they lose most of their effectiveness as bait also and should be replaced with fresh worms. It's true that sea worms are often difficult to obtain or expensive to use, but the salt-water angler who usually catches the most fish is the one who uses fresh worms and is not afraid to use plenty of worms. The stingy angler who cuts his worms into tiny pieces and keeps the dead worms on his hook for long periods of time is only reducing his chances of catching fish.

Chapter II

CLAMS, MUSSELS AND OYSTERS

RIGHT BEHIND THE SEA WORMS IN POPULARITY AS BAIT FOR SALT-WATER FISH are the clams. These bivalve mollusks are numerous in numbers and species along both the Atlantic and Pacific Coasts, where they are found living in the mud and sand of beaches, inlets, bays and ocean. They are sought not only for bait but also for food, and great quantities are shipped annually to various parts of the country to supply fish markets, restaurants, roadstands, canneries, bait dealers and fishing boats. Although there are many species of clams which can be used as bait, only those which are commonly used in fishing and are easily obtained can be dealt with here.

SURF CLAM

The surf clam (*Mactra solidissima*) is the largest bivalve found along the Atlantic Coast, sometimes reaching a length of 7 inches. It is also called the skimmer clam, hen clam, ocean clam, sea clam and giant clam. This clam lives in the sand in the surf along the ocean but is also found in deeper water up to 60 feet or so. Large quantities are dredged up to a mile offshore by commercial fishermen. The surf clam has a heavy shell and powerful foot which it uses to dig into the sand. In color the shell varies from yellowish white to gray or brown. This large clam is found from Labrador to North Carolina, but they are most numerous from New England to New Jersey. A smaller variety (*Mactra solidissima similis*) is more commonly found south of Cape Hatteras in southern waters. The surf clam or skimmer is the one usually sold for bait along the North Atlantic Coast and it is also used for food to a certain extent.

Surf clams can be bought from bait dealers, boat liveries and tackle stores in many areas. They can also be found by wading in shallow water at low tide along the sandy beaches where they can be noticed partly exposed in the sand. A few live clams can often be picked up lying high and dry on the beach at low tide. After a storm large quantities are often

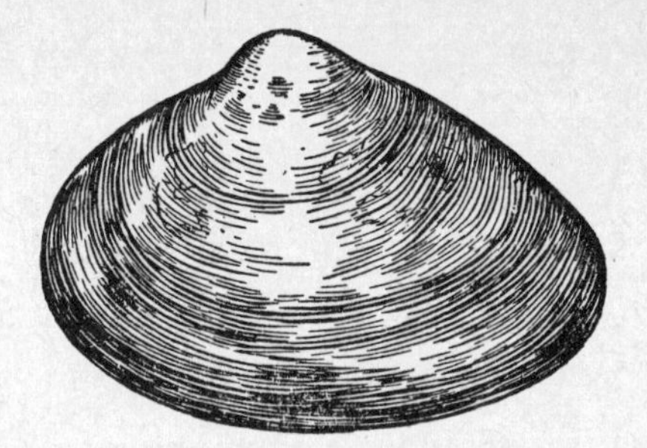

Surf Clam

washed up on the beach and can be gathered for future use. Surf clams are a favorite bait for striped bass, cod, haddock, sea bass, tautog or blackfish, scup or porgy and almost any other fish found in the ocean.

PISMO CLAM

The Pismo clam (*Tivela stultorum*) of the Pacific Coast is somewhat similar to the surf clam of the Atlantic Coast in that it is a large clam and prefers the surf-swept sandy beaches. It is found from Half Moon Bay near San Francisco to Mexico but is most numerous in California at Pismo Beach. It may reach 7 inches in length but most of the clams found run under 6 inches. It has a thick, heavy shiny shell which varies from pale brown to dark brown in color. Some Pismo clams also have lines and stripes forming patterns on the shell.

The Pismo clam is highly valued for food, and millions are dug each year for this purpose mostly by individuals, since commercial digging or selling of the clams is strictly regulated. Large numbers of the clams are also used for bait. Because of this great demand for bait and food, laws have been passed to protect the Pismo clams which are in danger of becoming extinct in many areas. These laws have open and closed seasons, protected areas, a bag limit and minimum size limit. A sport fishing license is also required to take the clams. Check your California game laws before you start digging Pismo clams for bait. If you dig out of season, take more clams than the law allows or use small clams under the minimum size limit you can be subject to a stiff fine.

Pismo clams can be obtained by digging on sandy beaches at low tide on the exposed flats or in water 3 or 4 feet deep. By probing with the fork you can feel when you strike a clam; then it can be uncovered. Sometimes you can notice the siphons of the clam slightly exposed under the water. On dry sandy beaches with the flats exposed at low tide, you may notice the holes and mounds of sand which often reveal the location of the clam. Another way to obtain the clams is to drag rakes with long handles either by hand or with a boat. Storms and heavy tides also wash the clams out of the sand and leave them stranded high and dry where they can be picked up. Whichever method is used in obtaining the clams, care should be taken with undersized clams which cannot be legally kept. The law states that these should be returned to deep water or the hole from which they are removed. Too many careless diggers toss these clams on the sand high and dry where they soon die.

Pismo clams are usually used for corbina, surf perch, croakers and flounders but will also catch many other fishes found in Pacific waters.

HARD SHELL CLAM

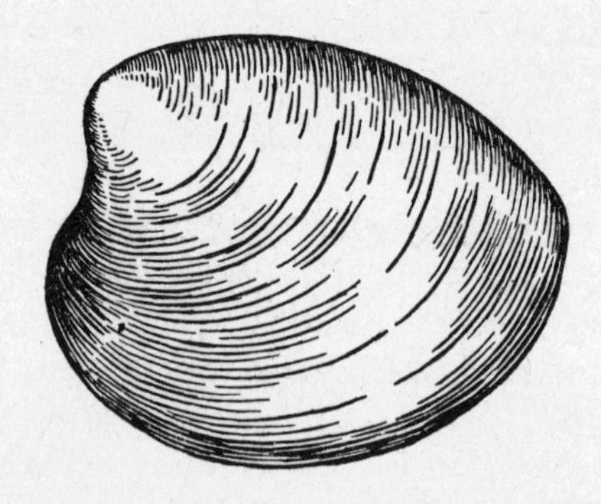

The hard shell clam (*Venus mercenaria*) is the common clam of the Atlantic Coast which is sold in fish markets and served in restaurants. It is also called the hard clam, round clam, little-neck clam, cherrystone clam and quahog, depending on its size and where it is found. The hard clam when fully grown may reach 6 inches in length but most specimens are 3 inches or less. In color it may be white, gray or yellowish on the outside with a violet border along the inside edge of the shell. The hard shell clam is found from Maine to Florida in the sandy and muddy bottoms of bays, sounds and other tidal waters. There are several related species and varieties of the hard shell clam found along the Atlantic and Gulf Coasts.

Millions of pounds of hard shell clams are taken annually by commercial fishermen, mostly by dredging or with tongs and rakes in fairly deep water. The angler can always buy his hard clams at a fish market or one of the roadside stands which sell the clams along the Atlantic Coast. They can also be obtained in shallow water by digging with clam hoes, rakes or forks in the sand and mud bottoms where the clams lie just under the surface.

Although hard shell clams are more commonly used for food than for bait, they can be used for cod, haddock, striped bass, porgies or scup, croakers, tautog or blackfish, flounders and many other salt-water fishes.

SOFT SHELL CLAM

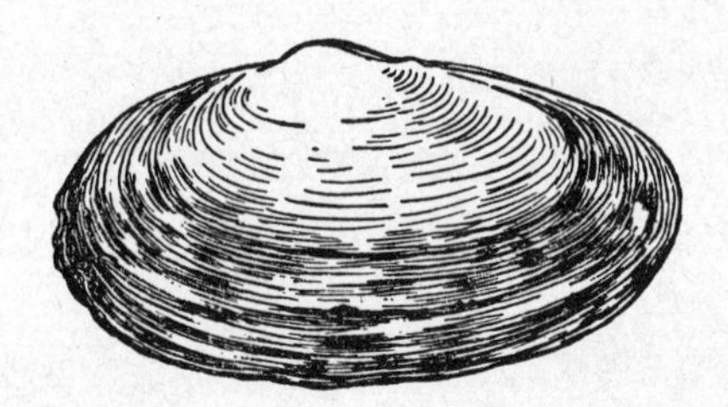

The soft shell clam (*Mya arenaria*) is another clam which is more popular as food than as bait. It is also called the soft clam, long clam, long-neck clam, mud clam, sand clam, steamer clam, nannynose and squirt clam. The soft shell clam may reach 5 inches in length but most of those found run 2 or 3 inches. This clam is easily recognized by its long siphon or neck and oval-shaped shell which is a dull gray or chalky white in color. It is usually found buried in muddy bottoms about a foot below the surface between high- and low-water tide marks. Soft shell clams are found from the Arctic Seas to North Carolina but are most numerous north of Cape Cod. These clams are also found along the Pacific Coast from British Columbia to Monterey, California. They are not native to this area, but were introduced to Pacific waters from the Atlantic many years ago.

Soft shell clams can be obtained on the tidal flats, where they lie buried, by digging with a clam hoe or garden fork. They can be located easily since they squirt a jet of water into the air if a person walks over the mud flats where they are found. Soft clams can also be bought in fish markets and at roadside stands near the seacoast.

The part of the soft clam which makes the best bait is the tough siphon which stays on the hook fairly well. The dark skin can be peeled off to make a more attractive bait. Soft shell clams will catch tautog or blackfish, eels, porgies or scup, flounders and many other salt-water fishes.

RAZOR AND JACKKNIFE CLAMS

There are many species of these long, cylindrical-shaped clams found along both the Atlantic and Pacific Coasts. Some are narrow and shaped like old-fashioned razors with square ends. Others are wider with shells that are rounded on the ends. A few razor clams may reach 10 inches in length, but most of them average between 2 and 6 inches. These clams live in the sand and mud flats of bays and ocean beaches where they lie buried beneath the surface.

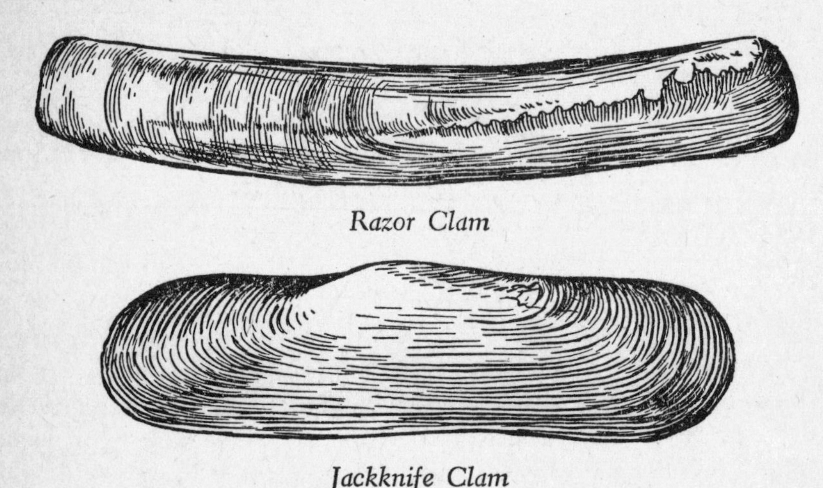

Razor Clam

Jackknife Clam

Razor and jackknife clams are not used too often for bait since they are not too easily obtained and are sold as bait only in a few areas. The most commonly used is the jackknife clam (*Tagelus californianus*), which is found from Santa Barbara to Mexico and is used by anglers in Southern California for spotfin croakers. It is also known as the California razor clam. But most of the other kinds of razor clams can be used for a wide variety of salt-water fishes.

Razor and jackknife clams can move with amazing speed through the sand or mud in which they are found. They should be dug quickly with narrow shovels before they go down too deep. Some anglers use special spears with an arrowhead on the end which they thrust into the burrows of the jackknife clams. The spear is pushed until the arrowhead passes the clam, then it is twisted and the clam closes on the shank of the spear and is pulled to the surface. It is also claimed that if you sprinkle some salt over the burrow in the mud or sand where the razor clams are living, they will quickly come to the surface.

OTHER CLAMS

There are many other kinds of clams which can be used for bait if they can be obtained in sufficient numbers and are large enough to make practical baits. Some of them are numerous enough to be sold for food but others are rarely dug by commercial clam diggers and can be obtained only by individual amateur diggers. The angler who wants to dig his own clams should check his local and state laws to see if there are any regulations governing the taking of these shellfish. Clams are protected in certain areas by open and closed seasons or areas, size limits and bag limits. You may have to be a resident of the area or need a license or permit to dig clams.

MUSSELS

These bivalves are familiar to all who go down to the ocean or bay at low tide, and are found clinging to the rocks, piles, mud flats and any other object below high-water mark. Mussels may be black, blue-black, brown or olive-colored depending on the species and where found. One of the

Edible Mussel

commonest mussels is the edible mussel (*Mytilus edulis*), also called the Atlantic mussel, blue mussel, sea mussel along the Atlantic Coast and bay mussel along the Pacific Coast. It may reach 3 inches in length but most of those found run from about an inch to 2½ inches. The edible mussel ranges from the Arctic seas to North Carolina along the Atlantic Coast and is also found in Europe and along the Pacific Coast, where it was introduced from the Atlantic many years ago.

Along the Pacific coast the large sea mussel (*Mytilus californianus*), which ranges from Alaska to Mexico, is commonly found attached to rocks between tide marks along the surf. These mussels, also called "big mussels," may reach 8 inches in length but average 3 or 4 inches.

Another common mussel along the Atlantic Coast is the ribbed mussel (*Modiolus demissus plicatulus*), which is also known as the mudbank mussel and fan mussel. It is found in bays on tidal flats and along the banks of tidal creeks and rivers. It is easily recognized by the grooves along its dull, olive or brownish shell. They reach 3 inches when fully grown but those usually found are much smaller.

Ribbed Mussel

There are many other species of mussels which are found in salt water which can be used for bait if they are large enough. Although mussels are somewhat difficult to keep on a hook the fact that they can be obtained easily makes them a favorite bait with some anglers. Mussels are usually so numerous in most places that they can be readily gathered from rocky shores, jetties, piles and mud flats where they are found anchored. They can also be bought in many coastal fish markets where they are sold for food. They will catch blackfish or tautog, flounders, croakers, corbina and many other salt-water fishes. Mussels can also be crushed and used in chum pots or just tossed overboard a few at a time to attract fish close to the boat or bank where an angler is fishing. They are also crushed and put into crab traps or minnow traps to attract crabs and baitfish.

OYSTERS

These popular bivalves as everyone knows are used for food more than for bait. But they can be used for many of the smaller bottom fishes in salt water such as flounders, blackfish or tautog, sheepshead, even though they are difficult to keep on the hook. Oysters are found along both coasts, and the common edible oyster (*Ostrea virginica*), usually found in restaurants and fish markets, is the most numerous along the Atlantic Coast and is also found along the Pacific Coast, where it was introduced from the Atlantic. The tree or coon oysters (*Ostrea frons*) are found growing on the roots of mangrove trees in southern waters. Oysters are gathered with dredges and tongs in deep water or by hand in shallow water.

SCALLOPS

This is another shellfish which is considered more of a food than a bait. But in this case you can have your bait and eat it too. For only the heavy muscle which holds the two shells together is eaten in this country and the rest is usually discarded. This remainder although somewhat soft can be used as bait for many of the same fishes which are caught on clams and mussels. Two kinds of scallops are usually found on the market. One is the sea scallop (*Pecten grandis*), which is one of the largest and is found

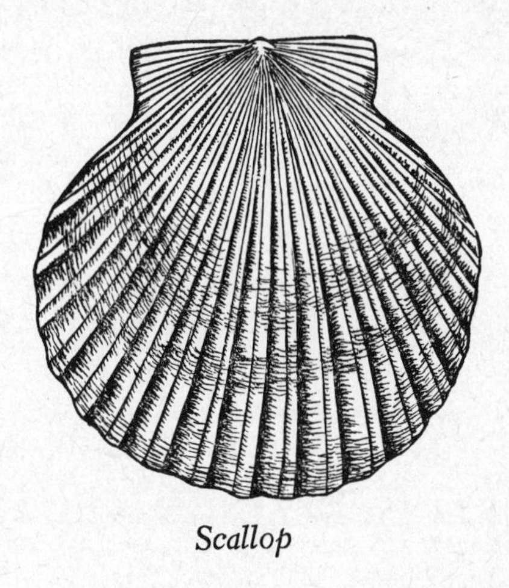

Scallop

in the ocean from New Jersey north to Labrador. The other is the bay scallop (*Pecten irradians*), which is found in inshore waters from New England to Florida. But there are many other species of scallops found along the Atlantic and Pacific Coasts. Scallops are rarely gathered by anglers solely for bait, but if you can find a place where scallop fishermen shuck or open the scallops to remove the muscle meat you can usually get the discarded shells with the remaining meat for the asking.

KEEPING AND HOOKING

After you have your clams, mussels or oysters you have the problem of keeping or preserving them for future use. They will stay alive in a cool spot away from the sun for quite a while. For long periods they can be kept in a bushel basket or wire cage or bait box submerged in salt water. Make sure that the water covers them most of the time and that they are not exposed to warm air, sunlight or rain for too long a period. Clams, mussels and oysters can also be kept on ice for several days.

To prepare clams, mussels or similar shellfish for bait they must be shucked or removed from their shells. This can be done by inserting a knife blade between the two shells and cutting the muscles which hold them together. But most anglers to save time, work and a possible injury to the hands just strike the clams or muscles with a hammer or rock, or against a hard object to crack the shells. This is usually done on the fishing grounds, but some anglers prefer to remove the meat from the shells and pack it in jars or other containers. When this is done the bait takes less space, weighs less and saves time for actual fishing. If you pack this meat in an airtight container and add plenty of salt you can keep the bait for some time, especially if you place it in an icebox or refrigerator when it is not in use. The salt will also toughen the bait a bit.

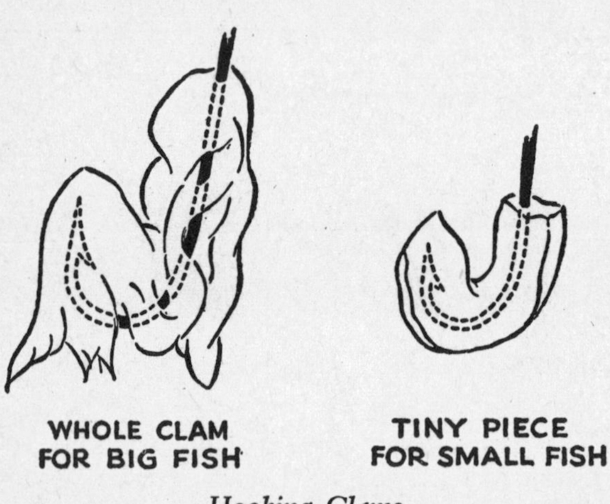

Hooking Clams

When it comes to hooking clams, mussels and similar bivalves you will find that not too much can be done to prevent fish from stealing the bait. Some anglers steam or scald their clams or mussels with boiling water to toughen them a bit. You can also open clams and mussels and let them lie in the air and sun for a while so that they will dry out and stay on the hook a little better. Wrapping the soft meat around the hook with fine thread will also help to hold it in place.

When hooking clams for big fish like striped bass or cod the meat from one or more large clams should be used. Surf clams or hard shell clams can be hooked first through the tough, muscular foot, then twisted and hooked once again; after this the softer portions should be hooked and draped around the bend and shank of the hook. The stringy mantle lying along the edge of the shell can also be used if it is pierced and wrapped around the hook several times. For smaller fish the muscular foot can be cut into sections and then hooked once or twice. In clams with long siphons like the soft shell clam this siphon is fairly tough and makes a good bait if the dark outer skin is peeled off. Mussels and oysters are even softer than clams and about the only way to keep them on the hook for any length of time is to wrap the soft meat around the hook with thread. For some fish like tautog and sheepshead, the small clams and mussels can be cracked and placed on the hook without removing the shell parts.

However, this very softness of the bait is attractive to salt-water fishes and you can't go wrong by taking along clams or other bivalves on your fishing trip.

Chapter III

SNAILS, WHELKS AND CONCHS

THIS SECTION WILL DEAL WITH SNAILS, WHELKS, CONCHS AND OTHER UNIvalve or single-shell mollusks used for bait. They are so numerous in numbers and species that only those which are commonly used for bait can be included.

MOON SNAILS

These are the large sea snails which are found buried in the sand or mud from shallow coastal waters to depths of more than 200 fathoms. There are several species found along both the Atlantic and Pacific Coasts and they are easily recognized by the typical snaillike appearance of the shells and the large meaty part or foot which spreads beyond the shell. Along the Atlantic Coast one of the largest is *Polinices heros*, also called the moon shell or sand-collar snail, and is 4 inches in diameter when fully grown. It can be found wholly or partly buried in sand or mud between tide marks and in shallow and deep water. It ranges from the Gulf of St. Lawrence to North Carolina. Another closely related moon shell or sand-collar snail is *Polinices duplicata*, which is found from Massachusetts to the Gulf of Mexico. It doesn't grow as large as the one mentioned above. On the Pacific Coast one of the largest is the Western moon snail (*Polinices lewisii*), also known as the Lewis moon snail. It may reach 5 inches in diameter and is found from British Columbia to San Diego, California.

The meaty part of the moon snails makes a tough bait which can be cut up and used for many bottom-feeding fish. It is used for codfish and can be placed on the same hook with a piece of clam, since it is not stolen so easily by smaller fish such as bergalls or cunners.

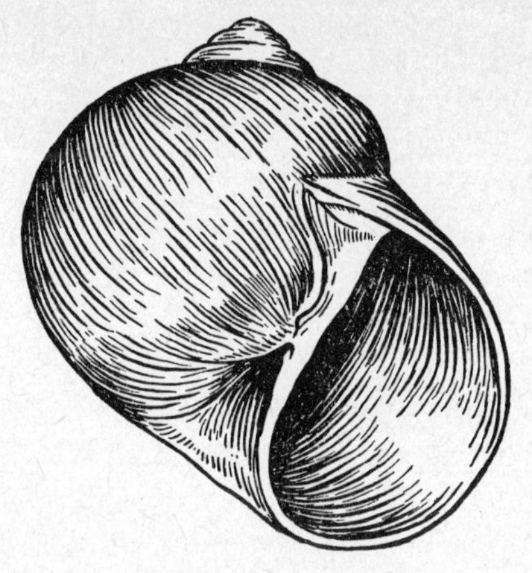

Moon Snail

PERIWINKLES

These are the common small sea snails which are seen by the thousands clinging to rocks, piles and seaweed in shallow water and high and dry between tide marks. The edible periwinkle (*Littorina litorea*), also called the common periwinkle, shore periwinkle and winkle, is the most numer-

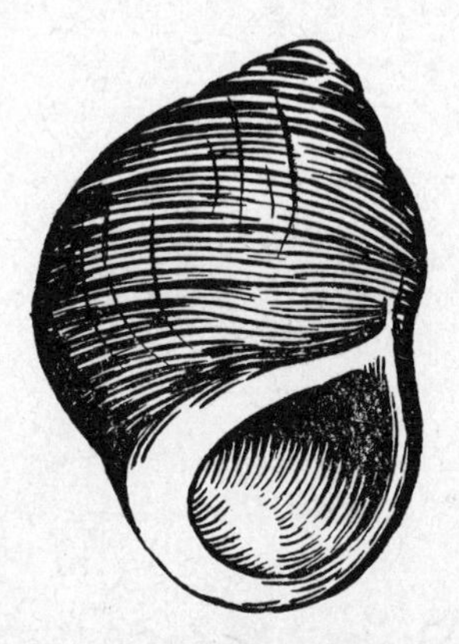

Edible Periwinkle

ous in New England along the seashore. It prefers rocky areas from Labrador to Delaware Bay. It has a shell which varies in color being black, olive-green, brownish-yellow or gray often banded with brown. This periwinkle is commonly eaten and used for bait in Europe, from where it was introduced to Canada and then spread southward along the Atlantic Coast. It is also eaten and used as bait to a certain extent in the United States. Although it is somewhat small it can be cracked and the meat removed and placed on a hook. Several periwinkles can be strung on the same hook to make a larger bait. Periwinkles can be used for many of the smaller bottom feeding fishes such as tautog and porgies.

There are many other kinds of periwinkles found along both the Atlantic and Pacific Coasts which can be used for bait. Many of them are too small to make practical baits but others are large enough to be used. The good thing about periwinkles is that they make a fine emergency bait. They are almost always available in such numbers that when you run out of bait you can gather all you need with little effort.

WHELKS

The whelks are the largest univalve shells found north of Cape Hatteras along the Atlantic Coast. The waved whelk (*Buccinum undatum*), also called the common whelk and English whelk, has long been used for food

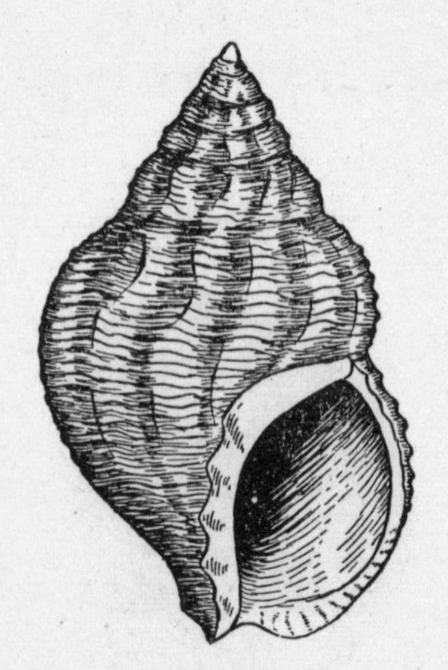

Waved Whelk

in Europe and as bait in the cod fisheries. It reaches from 2 to 4 inches in length and is brownish in color. Along the Atlantic Coast it is found from Labrador to New Jersey. Along its northern range it is found close to shore but farther south it stays in deep water.

Another group of whelks are the neptune shells, and here one of the commonest is the channeled whelk (*Busycon canaliculatum*), also called the conch or winkle, and is found from Cape Cod to northern Florida. It reaches from 6 to 9 inches in length and prefers a sandy bottom in shallow water. Another whelk is the knobbed whelk (*Busycon caricum*), also called the giant whelk, pear conch, conch or winkle. It is the largest of the Atlantic Coast whelks sometimes reaching 10 inches in length. It is easily separated from the channeled whelk since it has a row of knobs on the shoulder near the top of the shell. It is found from Cape Cod to Florida. South of North Carolina to Texas another whelk, the left-handed whelk (*Busycon perversum*), also called the lightning shell, is the species usually found. There are many other kinds of whelks found along the Atlantic and Pacific Coasts and most of the larger ones can be used for bait.

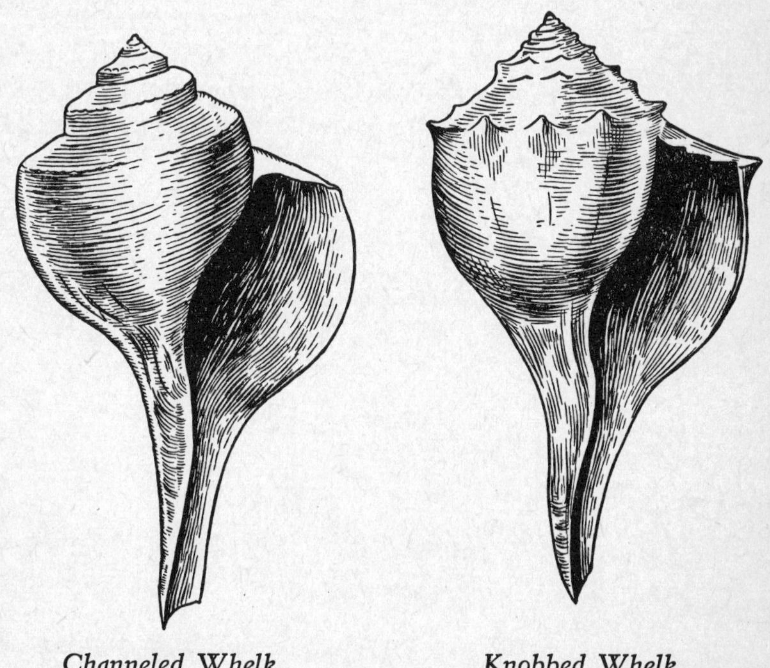

Channeled Whelk *Knobbed Whelk*

Sometimes whelks can be bought in fish markets or from bait dealers, but usually you'll have to obtain your own. Those that are found in very deep water are taken by commercial fishermen. In waters of moderate depth some whelks can be caught by leaving dead fish or crushed shellfish in wire traps over night. The whelks will crawl into the trap and can be hauled out in the morning. In shallow water you can often gather some of the whelks by wading or diving for them. A few may be washed high and dry on the beach or stranded in tidal pools and can be picked up.

Whelks make a tough bait and are often used for cod either alone or together with softer baits like clam. The pests like bergalls or cunners will quickly steal the clam bait but have a hard time with the whelks. Thus the angler can be fairly sure that his hook always has some bait on it, and he doesn't have to haul in and look at it too often. In fact, the whelks are so tough that many anglers pound them with a wooden mallet or other instrument to soften them up a bit, and also to allow the fluid to ooze out. Whelks can also be cut up into tiny pieces and used for fish like tautog or blackfish, porgy or scup, sea bass and many other bottom fishes.

CONCHS

The conchs are another group of very large sea snails which are used for bait in tropical waters. One of the largest is the giant conch (*Strombus gigas*), also called the queen conch, white conch and fountain shell. It is a very large shell which may reach a foot in length and weigh five pounds.

Giant Conch

The beautiful pink and white shells are often seen for sale in curio shops and in homes on mantels. This conch is found in the southern tip of Florida, the Bahamas and West Indies, where it crawls around on the ocean bottom and coral reefs. Many other species of conchs are found in tropical waters. One of these, the Florida conch (*Strombus pugilis alatus*) is found from Cape Hatteras to the Gulf of Mexico and is quite common in the shallow waters of Florida.

Conchs are usually caught by diving for them in shallow water. But at times you can capture a good supply by lowering a basket or trap filled with dead fish or meat and leaving it there to attract the conchs. In some areas they are popular as food, but anglers consider them more important as bait for fish such as bonefish, groupers, grunts and snappers. The conch meat is also cut or ground up and thrown overboard as chum to attract various fishes.

LIMPETS

The limpets, which are small univalve shells shaped like cones and are found attached to rocks in between tide marks or in shallow water, are sometimes used for bait. There are many kinds found along the Atlantic and Pacific Coasts. One species used on the West Coast is the white-cap limpet (*Acmaea mitra*) which has a high, white conical shell which may be an inch in height. Limpets are well camouflaged and resemble their surroundings and are hard to see. They cling to the rocks tightly but can be removed by slipping a thin knife blade quickly under the shell.

Most of the snails, whelks and conchs can be kept for several days like clams in a cool spot or on ice. Or they can be suspended in wire cages or similar containers in salt water. The snails, whelks and conchs can be opened with a hammer or hatchet. But if these tools are lacking the shells can be hit against one another or some hard object. A knife is useful in extracting the meat from the shell and for cutting it up into pieces of the right size. A club or wooden mallet is also handy for pounding the tough meat to make it a softer and better bait. Conchs can be baited like clams except that you only have to hook them once or twice to keep them on the hook.

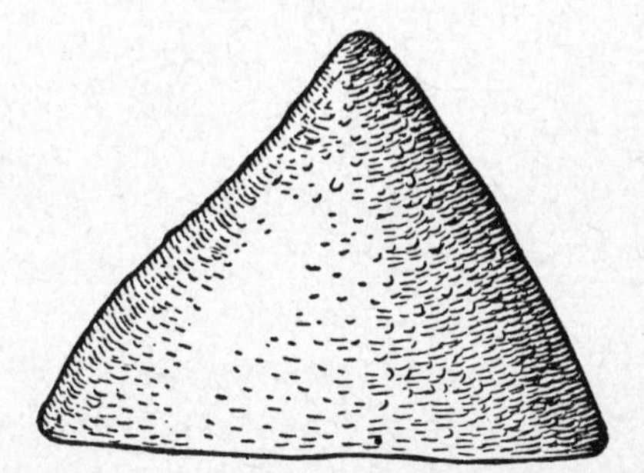

White-Cap Limpet

Of course, the list of snaillike baits above is far from complete and there are many others which can be used for bait. Almost any shellfish which is large enough and can be gathered in sufficient quantities can be cracked open and tried for bait. You will generally find that they will take some kind of salt-water fish.

Chapter IV

SQUID AND OCTOPUS

ALTHOUGH SQUIDS AND OCTOPUSES ARE CONSIDERED MOLLUSKS LIKE CLAMS, mussels, oysters and other shellfish by scientists, they are so unique in structure and habits and so important as bait that they rate a special section. Millions of pounds of squid are used each year by commercial fishermen and anglers, especially in the North Atlantic. They are also popular as food in many countries and to a certain extent in this country among people of Oriental or Mediterranean descent.

The common Atlantic squid (*Loligo pealii*), also called the blunt-tailed squid and inkfish, is so strange in appearance that it is easily recognized. The long, round body, which tapers to the tail end and has two fins, has an opening on the opposite end into which the head fits. The head has two, large staring eyes and ten tentacles or arms which surround a black, parrotlike beak which is the mouth. Squid swim backward very rapidly by squirting out a stream of water from a siphon found under the neck. When alive the squid varies in color changing rapidly into different blends and tints of red, brown, yellow, green or blue, depending on its reactions and surroundings. When dead the squid turns white.

The common Atlantic squid usually averages 5 to 8 inches in body length and is found from Massachusetts Bay to South Carolina from the shore line to depths of 50 fathoms. It is rare north of Cape Cod where the short-tailed squid (*Ommastrephes illecebrosus*), also called the sea arrow or flying squid, is the one more commonly found. This squid has shorter fins than the common squid and is usually found in deeper water from the Bay of Fundy to New Jersey. There are several other species of squid found along the Atlantic Coast, from tiny 2 or 3 inchers to the giant squid which may reach more than 50 feet in over-all length.

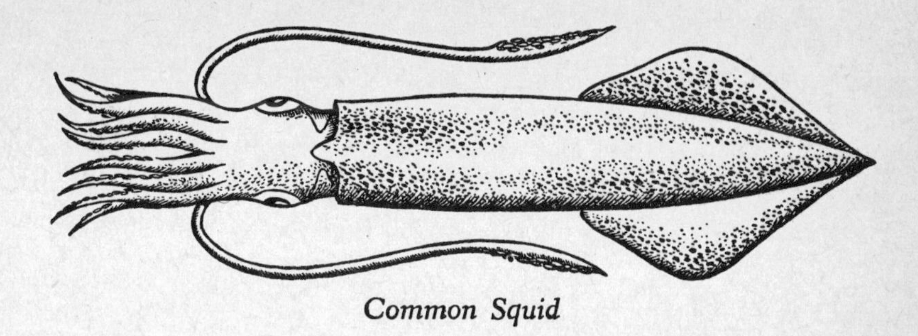

Common Squid

Along the Pacific Coast the common squid is *Loligo opalescens*, which ranges from Puget Sound to San Diego and reaches an over-all length of about a foot. Other species of squid found in the Pacific run from tiny 2-inch specimens to giants measuring several feet.

OBTAINING, KEEPING AND HOOKING

During certain years squid are scarce, while in others they are abundant, but commercial fish houses, fish markets and bait dealers usually have some for sale either fresh or frozen. Squid are usually taken by commercial fishermen in traps, pound nets, otter trawls or haul seines. But during certain seasons and in some areas squid come close to shore, espe-

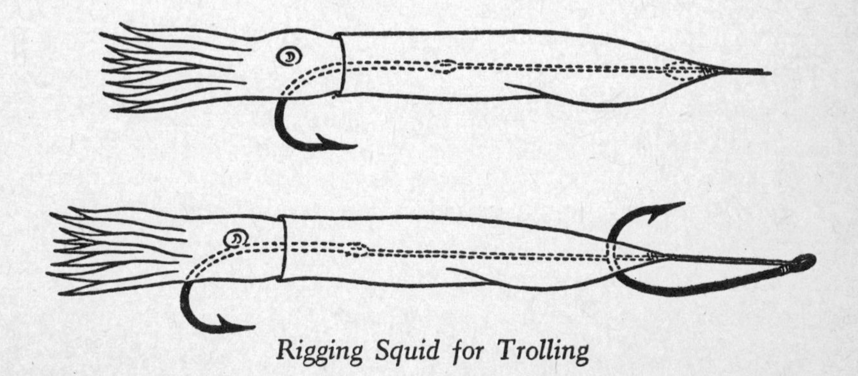

Rigging Squid for Trolling

cially at night, and these can often be caught from boats or from land or piers with seines or dip nets. A light on a boat or pier or shore will attract small baitfish and the squid will often gather to feed on them.

Squid are also sometimes stranded on shore in large numbers and can be picked up, especially late at night or early in the morning. Squid can also be snagged with one or more treble hooks on the end of a line if the hooks are baited with one or two shiny baitfish. The hooks and bait should be moved to attract the attention of the squid and when it tries to envelope the bait a quick jerk on the line will often hook it.

Squid are difficult to keep alive in captivity since they require a lot of room and plenty of salt water. They are rarely used in the live state unless they are caught and placed on the hook as soon as possible. Most of the squid are frozen or are kept on ice or in a refrigerator until used. They can also be cleaned, washed, cut up and packed in containers or jars with plenty of salt and kept in a cool place for quite a while.

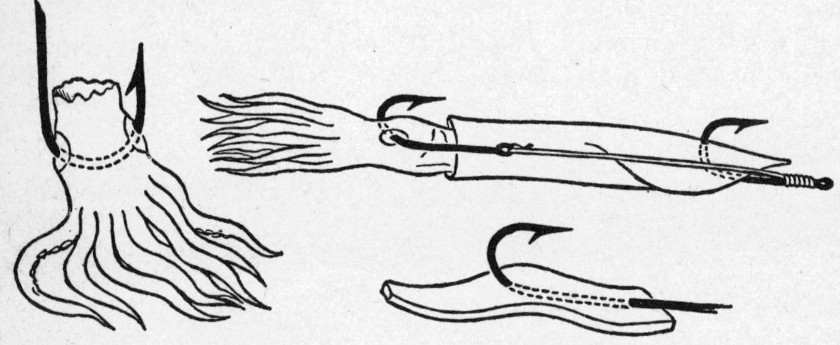

Hooking Squid for Bottom Fishing

The whole squid is a favorite bait for swordfish and is also used for some of the marlins, tunas and striped bass. For these fish the squid is usually used with one or two large hooks. The simplest way is to hook the squid once through the tail with a single hook. Another method is to run the single hook through the center of the squid with the bend and point coming out at the head or mouth. When using two hooks one hook is run through the body and comes out at the head or side, while the other hook is run through the tail section. A flexible wire leader can be used to connect both hooks. To prevent the tail of the squid from sliding down the leader a ball of string is often wrapped around the leader just inside the tail section of the squid to help hold it in position.

An emergency rig often used for striped bass is to bend back the barbs on two hooks and slip the eye of the second hook over the first and the eye of a third hook over the second hook so that you have a series of three hooks lined up. The squid is then hooked so that the first hook with the eye to which the leader is tied runs through the tail section of the squid; the center hook runs through the body and the last hook pierces the head. In all these methods the tail section is always nearest the leader so that the squid rides backward when trolled or retrieved during a cast.

Some anglers also use a half-round lead weight which is hammered or soldered onto the shank of a hook just below the eye. Then the tail end of the squid is cut off slightly and the fins are removed so that the squid can be threaded on the shank of the hook. The tail end is then tied flush against the lead weight, producing a squid bait which can be cast more easily and also trolled.

When bottom fishing for striped bass, cod, channel bass, large weakfish and bluefish, a small whole squid or large portions are used. The head with tentacles left on (the two longest ones can be cut off) makes a good bait for striped bass. So does the body section. Pieces of squid are often used together with clams or other soft baits on the same hook. The soft baits are often stolen by the fish but the tough squid usually remains. The snow-white color of the squid also makes a more attractive bait than most other baits.

For smaller fish such as the porgy or scup, sea bass, pollack, fluke or summer flounder, either triangular or rectangular strips anywhere from 1 to 4 inches long are generally used. Long, narrow strips of squid are sometimes used like pork rind in conjunction with artificial lures such as plugs, spoons, feather lures and spinners when casting or trolling. The squid makes a tough bait and all you have to do is pierce it once or twice with a hook and it will stay on for a long time.

OCTOPUS

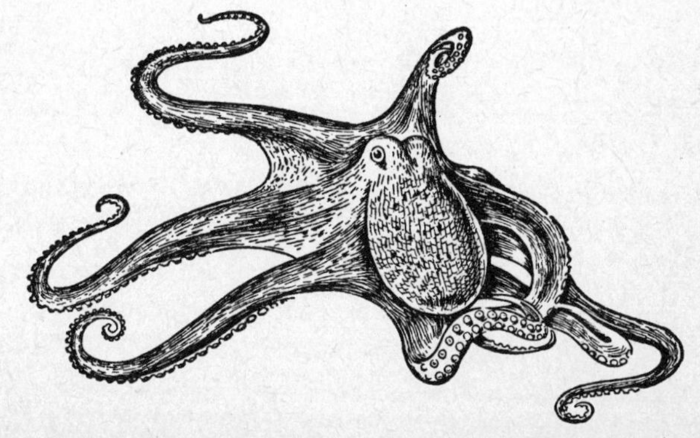

This close relative of the squid can also be used for bait in many areas where it is found. Along the Atlantic Coast the octopus is not commonly found in northern waters. In the warmer waters of Florida, Bermuda and points farther south they are more numerous. In the Pacific Ocean various species of octopuses are more common, being found from Alaska to tropical waters. Although most of them, especially the larger specimens, prefer deep water some are found in shallow water. These can often be caught by turning over rocks in shallow water or pools or probing with a gaff hook or spear into crevices or holes around reefs and rocks. The entrances to octopus dens are often littered with the remains of crabs and shellfish on which they feed. They can also be caught in traps with small funnel openings baited with dead fish or crabs.

The octopus makes a tough bait and the whole ones have been used for swordfish, while the tentacles which are split open and cut up into small sections are used for many salt-water fishes. If the skin is peeled off and the meat is pounded to soften it, the result is a more attractive bait.

Chapter V

CRABS

THE CRABS ARE VERY NUMEROUS BOTH IN SPECIES AND NUMBERS IN THE SALT waters of the world. The Atlantic and Pacific shores of the United States have their share of these crustaceans which are eaten by many salt-water fishes. This despite the fact that most crabs are equipped with tough shells and pincers for protection. However, crabs do have periods when they are soft and helpless and this is when they usually make the best bait.

Before we take up the different kinds of crabs individually perhaps it would be helpful to explain the various stages in which crabs are found. Crabs shed their hard covering at intervals as they grow, to make room for the increase in size. Just before they shed their hard covering they are known as "shedder" or "peeler" crabs. To tell if you have a shedder, try breaking off one of the moving pincers on the large claws or one of the points found on each end of the top shell. If it breaks with difficulty and leaves no meat exposed it's a hard crab. If the shell breaks readily and leaves the soft, newly-formed meat of the new shell exposed, the crab is a shedder. After they shed their shells they are "soft shell" crabs, and when their new shell starts to harden but still caves in when pressed, they are called buckrams, leather-backs or paper-backs. Finally the shell hardens and they are hard shell crabs again. Crabs are used for bait in all their stages, but those which are in the soft shell or shedder stage are usually preferred.

BLUE CRAB

Of all the crabs found along the Atlantic Coast, the blue crab (*Callinectes sapidus*), also called the common edible crab, blue-claw crab and sea crab, is the most popular for food and bait. This is the crab which is usually sold in the fish markets and served in the restaurants in the hard or soft shell stages. It is found from Cape Cod to Florida and around the Gulf of Mexico to the Mississippi. The blue crab is easily recognized by its large size, the dark green back, white belly and long claws which are bright blue, blending into red at the tips. It reaches 6 inches or more in breadth along the top shell. It is a swimming crab and the hind legs are shaped like paddles to propel it through the water.

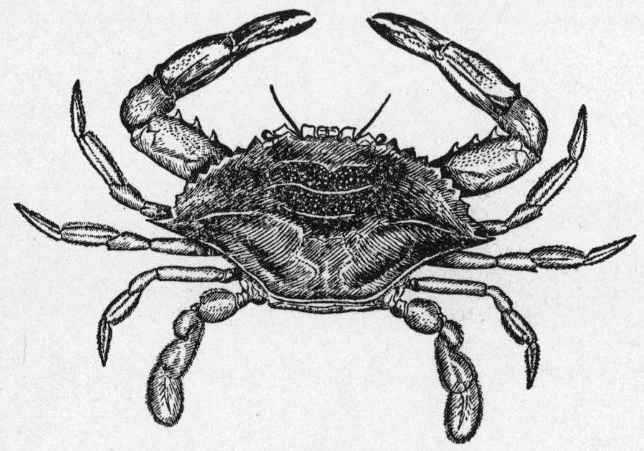

Blue Crab

Blue crabs are found in the salt and brackish waters of bays, sounds and rivers, where they prefer muddy bottoms covered with eel grass or sea lettuce. They are most active and numerous from May to October when they frequent the shallower waters. During the winter they move off into deep water.

Although blue crabs can be bought in the hard and soft shell stages in many fish markets and from commercial fishermen and bait dealers, many anglers prefer to catch their own. Shedder crabs are also sold by bait dealers but they are usually high in price.

Hard blue crabs can be captured in fairly large quantities by means of traps. The standard crab trap is the wire-box type in which the four sides fall open when the trap is on the bottom. When the trap is raised the four sides close, capturing any crabs which entered to feed on the dead fish or meat which is tied in the center of the contraption. This type of trap can be bought in many fishing-tackle and hardware stores along the seacoast. Another kind of trap used for crabs can be made from wire mesh in the shape of a bag. The open end is fairly wide, while the closed end is flattened. A line is tied to the open end or entrance and this trap can be baited with crushed clams or mussels to attract the crabs. These two traps can be used from bridges, piers, jetties or the shore where the water is fairly deep. If you use more than one trap you can usually obtain enough crabs in a short time. However, most of these will be hard crabs as not many shedder or soft crabs enter the traps.

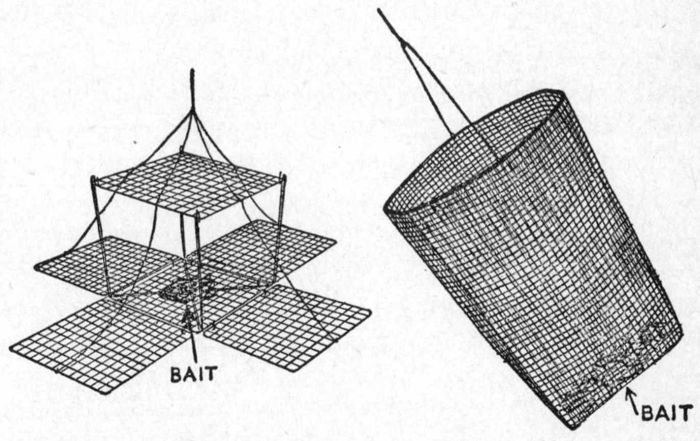

Two Types of Crab Traps

One of the best ways to obtain shedder or soft crabs is to wade in shallow water on the tidal flats and scoop up the crabs with a long-handled crab net. At first you may have difficulty in spotting the crabs among the eel grass and sea lettuce, but soon you'll see them either moving around or partly hidden under the weeds. And it will take a while to catch on to their tricky maneuverings before you are able to capture them in the net consistently. Many of these crabs will also be hard ones, but you will often find a shedder crab or soft shell hidden among the weeds. If you see one crab carrying another one you will usually find that the one underneath is either a shedder or soft shell crab.

A variation of the method above is to use a rowboat with one man slowly rowing or poling and another one in the bow of the boat with a crab net ready to scoop up the crabs. This method has the advantage of covering more territory and can be used in deeper water around piers, railroad trestles and bridges. The crabs are usually more plentiful at night when they come out of hiding and can be easily seen in the water with the help of a flashlight. Usually the best time to go crabbing with a dip net is during low tide when the water is shallower and the crabs are concentrated in smaller areas.

Another way you can capture hard blue crabs in small quantities is to tie a piece of fish or fish head to a string and lower it into the water. When a crab starts eating the bait he can usually be drawn slowly toward shore or the surface of the water and eased over a net, then scooped up.

When crabbing only the larger blue crabs should be kept for bait. In fact, some states have laws which prohibit the taking and keeping of blue crabs under a certain size. The female crabs carrying eggs are also protected in most states. The best policy is to check your local laws before you go after blue crabs.

Hard blue crabs will live for quite a while out of the water if they are kept in large containers away from the sun in a cool spot. For longer periods they can be kept in large floating boxes or bait cars in the water. Shedder crabs and soft shell crabs can be packed in one layer in seaweed, moss, straw or grass in a tray and kept on ice for several days. But separate containers should always be used for hard crabs, shedder crabs and soft-shell crabs.

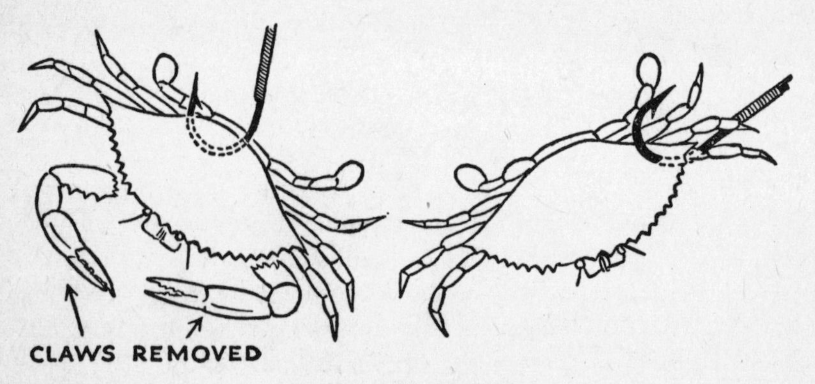

Hooking Hard Crab

To hook large, whole, hard blue crabs for big fish such as tarpon for bottom fishing the best method is to keep the crab alive. The large claws or pincers can be broken off and the hook should be run through the edge of the top shell from the bottom up. This should be done carefully in order not to crack the shell or make too big a hole. Another method is to remove one of the walking legs and insert the point of the hook into the hole left there and then curve the hook around and let the point and barb emerge between the other legs. The hard crabs can also be secured to the hook by tying them with thread.

When preparing shedder crabs the big claws should be removed and these can be cracked open and the meat inside is used for bait. Then remove the top shell by inserting your thumbnail under it in the back part of the crab. Now the crab can be turned over, and using a hard instrument like a knife handle hit the remaining shell on the belly in several places to crack it into small sections. These pieces of shell should then be peeled off leaving the soft body of the crab. The remaining legs should be cut or twisted off. If you are fishing for big fish the whole body of the crab can be used. For smaller fish or if you are short of bait you can cut the crab in half or in quarters. The same thing can be done with a soft shell crab which has already cast off its hard covering. The shedder and soft shell crabs are rather delicate baits and are hard to keep on a hook. The hook should be inserted two, three or more times into the portion used and twisted each time to help it stay on. Many salt-water anglers use fine thread to tie the crabs around the hook.

Blue crabs in the hard shell stage are used whole for tarpon and can be cut up for blackfish or tautog. In the soft or shedder stages they make good bait for striped bass, channel bass, weakfish, bluefish, cod, flounders, croakers and many other salt-water fishes.

LADY CRAB

The lady crab (*Ovalipes ocellatus*) is another swimming crab which is often used for bait, especially in surf fishing. It is found along the sandy beaches and inlets from Cape Cod to the Gulf of Mexico. It is easily recognized by its over-all yellow color and the purplish or reddish spots on its back. The shell, which is somewhat circular, reaches 3 inches in breadth and length. This crab is also called the calico crab, sand crab and speckled crab.

The lady crab can swim efficiently with its two paddles but is usually found crawling along the sandy bottom. When approached it buries itself in the sand leaving only the eye-stalks protruding. If they can be seen crawling around, lady crabs can be caught at low tide with a regular crab net and scooped up before they disappear in the sand. When the crabs cannot be seen they can often be caught by raking the area to dig them out. An ordinary garden rake can be used for this purpose if you attach a wire basket into which the crabs will fall. This wire basket is attached with the opening facing the teeth of the rake. When the rake is pulled through the soft sand, you can usually feel the crab strike the teeth; then you twist the handle of the rake quickly and the crab will fall into the wire basket. Sometimes the crab will be impaled on the teeth of the rake.

Like the blue crabs, the best lady crabs for bait are the shedder or soft shelled ones. But the small, hard lady crabs with shells about the size of half-dollars are often used, since they are not as thick as on the older and larger crabs. Lady crabs can be kept, prepared and hooked like blue crabs. They are especially popular as bait for striped bass, but will take weakfish, channel bass, cod, kingfish or northern whiting and many other salt-water fishes.

GREEN CRAB

Although the green crab (*Carcinides maenas*) is also considered a swimming crab like the blue crab and calico crab, it lacks the two swimming paddles and is mostly a crawling or running crab. It is common from Maine to New Jersey, especially in New England waters. The green crab is a small crab with the shell reaching about 3 inches in width and 2 inches in length. In color it is a dark, drab green spotted with yellow or yellow-green.

The green crab is most numerous in rocky areas where it is found between the tide marks or in shallow water or pools hiding under rocks, in crevices or in the seaweed. They can often be seen in tidal pools at low water. To obtain them, you can turn over the loose stones between tide marks or in the shallow water. In tidal pools they will often emerge from their hiding places if you throw some crushed mussels, clams or other shellfish into the water. Or you can tie a dead fish to a string and when the crabs come out to eat it you can catch them by hand or with a small dip net. To obtain green crabs in large quantities construct a wire trap with one or two funnel entrances similar to the minnow traps, but with larger openings. These, of course, must be baited with dead fish, crushed mussels, clams or other bait.

Green crabs are hardy and will live for days out of the water if kept in a cool spot. Or they can be kept in the live boxes submerged in the water like blue crabs. Crabs of about the same size should be kept in the same container.

Although green crabs are also found in the soft and shedder stages, they are usually used for bait in the hard stage and mostly for the tautog or blackfish. The larger crabs can be cut in half or quarters, while the smaller ones are used whole. The large pincer claws are usually removed before baiting the hook. The crabs stay on best if the hook is run between the legs or through the body and then into one of the legs.

FIDDLER CRABS

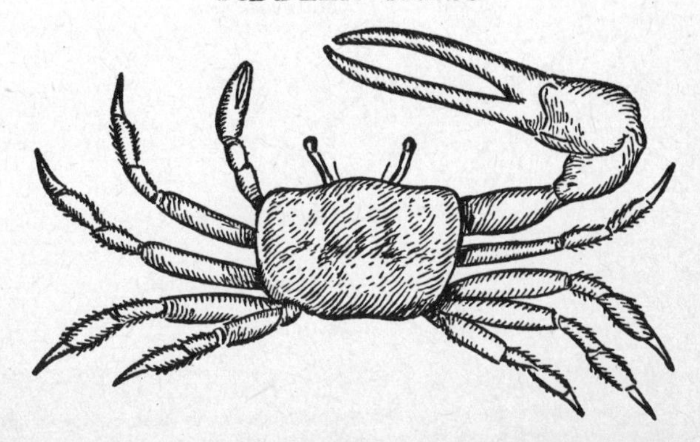

These small crabs are easily recognized because the males have one large claw and also because they live in sand or mud burrows along salt marshes or brackish bays. Three species are commonly found along the Atlantic Coast from Cape Cod to Florida. One of the most numerous is the mud fiddler (*Uca pugnax*), also called the marsh fiddler. It is olive or dark green in color with yellowish claws. It prefers the mud flats of bays where it digs burrows in the sedge banks.

Another fiddler crab often used for bait is the sand fiddler (*Uca pugilator*), also called the china-back fiddler. It grows somewhat larger than the mud fiddler and is much lighter in color, having a shiny, gray back with markings of brown, dark gray or violet. The claws are whitish or pale yellow. Although it is often found living in bays together with the mud fiddler it usually digs its burrows in sandier soil. It is preferred by most fishermen for bait.

The largest of the three fiddlers found from Cape Cod to Florida is the red-jointed fiddler (*Uca minax*), also called the soldier crab, a name often applied to the other species of fiddlers and hermit crabs. It is easily recognized by the red marks at the joints of the large claw and the gray or brown color of its shell. It prefers marshes in brackish or almost fresh waters where it digs holes above high-water mark.

On the Pacific Coast, the two species of fiddler crabs usually found are *Uca crenulata*, which ranges from San Diego south, and *Uca musica*, which is found from Mexico to Canada. They burrow in the salt marshes like the Atlantic Coast fiddlers.

Hooking Fiddler Crab

Fiddler crabs are often sold by bait dealers but the supply is somewhat undependable and many anglers obtain their own. Those that live in shallow burrows can be dug up with a clam hoe or fork. Where they are numerous they can often be herded into a trap which can be set up quickly and easily with some boards, fine mesh wire or cloth netting. This can be shaped like a corner or funnel and the fiddlers can be driven into it and then scooped up. After fiddler crabs disappear into their burrows they will emerge again in 10 or 15 minutes if you stay still and avoid making quick movements.

Fiddler crabs will usually live for several days in a box or other large container if it is kept in a cool spot. They should never be packed so tightly that they are on top of one another if you want to keep them for any length of time. However, if they are going to be used soon, then there is no harm in packing them closely in small containers.

To hook fiddler crabs remove the large claw for best results. Then you can run the point and barb of the hook into the hole where the big claw was attached and thread the crab as far up the hook as it will go. Another way is to force the point and barb of the hook up to the bend between the crab's legs. Still another way is to run the hook from the underside of the crab, through the body and out through the top shell.

Fiddler crabs are favorite baits for tautog or blackfish and sheepshead, but they will also take many other salt-water fishes which feed on crabs.

HERMIT CRABS

These crabs which live in empty snail shells are familiar to everyone who has gone down to the seashore where the smaller kinds are often numerous in shallow water. There are many species of hermit crabs found in Atlantic and Pacific waters. Some live in deep water, others prefer shallow water and a few in the tropics live on land.

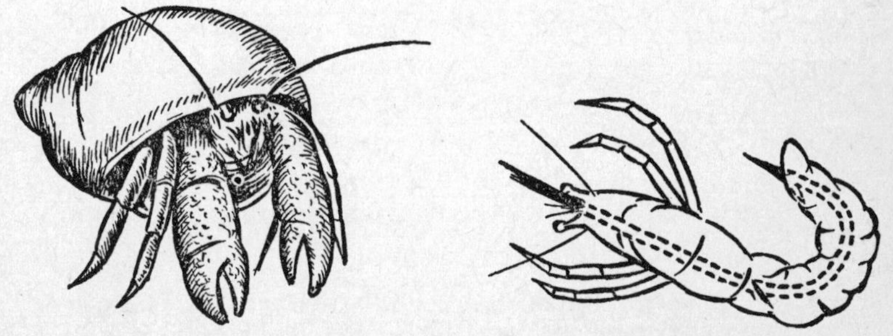

Hermit Crab and Method of Hooking

Along the Atlantic Coast one of the commonest hermit crabs is the small hermit crab (*Pagurus longicarpus*), which reaches only about an inch in length and is usually found occupying the shells of the smaller periwinkles or snails. It is very abundant in quiet shallow waters and tidal pools from Massachusetts to Florida. A larger species (*Pagurus pollicaris*), which is light red or brown and lives in empty whelk and moon shells, is known as the big hermit crab. It is found from Maine to Florida and prefers rocky and shelly bottoms of bays and sounds. North of Cape Cod a large, bright red species of hermit (*Pagurus bernhardus*) is found in deeper waters.

In tropical waters one of the largest hermits is the sea soldier (*Petrochirus bahamensis*), which when fully grown is often found occupying large conch shells. Another large hermit crab is the soldier crab (*Cenobita diogenes*), which is found in Florida and the West Indies living on land most of the time, except during the breeding season when they return to the water. They are sometimes found far inland dragging around their shell homes which are magpie shells.

Along the Pacific coast one of the commonest hermit crabs found in tide pools is *Pagurus samuelis*. Another species is *Pagurus granosimanus*, which is most numerous north of Puget Sound. And the hairy hermit (*Pagurus hirsutiusculus*) is another crab often found along the West Coast. All three of these hermits have an extreme range from Alaska to Lower California, but each species has a certain region where it is most abundant.

Of course, there are many other species of hermit crabs found along the Pacific and Atlantic Coasts which make just as good bait as those mentioned above. Those that are most numerous and can be gathered with ease are the ones which usually find their way into the salt-water angler's bait container.

Hermit crabs can be picked up easily in shallow water or on land when they are needed for bait. Sometimes they can be attracted in fairly large numbers by baiting the area with dead fish, crushed clams or similar food. At other times large numbers of hermit crabs are washed ashore by storms.

The sea-dwelling hermit crabs will stay alive for quite a while in their shell homes if they are kept in a cool spot out of the sun. They can be kept for longer periods in bait cars or other containers submerged in the water. Of course, the land-dwelling hermits will live out of the water for a long time.

When hermit crabs are used for bait they must be removed from their shell homes. This can be done by cracking the shell with a rock or other hard instrument. A lighted match or other heat applied to the shell will also bring the crab out of its home. The large claws of the hermit are removed before the crab is placed on the hook. When the whole hermit crab is used, the hook can be run through the entire body starting from the hard head and into the soft tail portion. Or you can pierce the hard body and then run the hook through the tail. For small fish the soft abdomen or tail alone can be used. Hermit crabs are good for bonefish, sheepshead, blackfish or tautog, permit, snappers and most any other salt-water fish that eats crabs.

OTHER CRABS

Some of the other crabs which can be used for bait at times include the many species which belong to the genus *Cancer* and are found along both the Atlantic and Pacific Coasts. They are often called rock crabs, edible crabs or market crabs. Along the Atlantic Coast the two species usually found are the rock crab (*Cancer irroratus*) and the Jonah crab or northern crab (*Cancer borealis*). Along the Pacific Coast *Cancer magister* and *Cancer antennarus* are the ones commonly found. These crabs, as their name implies, live among rocks although they may also bury themselves partly in the sand. Most of them are some shade of yellowish- or reddish-brown and most of them are edible. In shallow water they can be picked up by hand or in a crab net. But in deeper water special crab traps baited with dead fish are usually used.

Then there is the ghost crab (*Ocypoda albicans*), also called the sand crab, which is found from New Jersey south along the Atlantic Coast. It lives in burrows along sandy beaches near and above high-water mark. These crabs are fast runners and very difficult to catch especially during the daytime. But at night when they are more numerous they can often be blinded by a flashlight or trapped some distance from their burrows.

The large stone crab (*Menippe mercenaria*) can be used for bait in Florida and other southern waters where it is found. But this crab is so popular for food that it is now scarce and you cannot depend on obtaining it in sufficient numbers to use for bait.

Of course, there are many other crabs both large and small found along the Atlantic and Pacific Coasts which can be used for bait. Just because a crab is not listed here does not mean that it cannot be used for bait. Try any crab which can be obtained in the area you are fishing and you will generally find that some kind of fish will take it.

Chapter VI

SHRIMPS AND OTHER CRUSTACEANS

ALTHOUGH THE SHRIMPS AND OTHER CRUSTACEANS DEALT WITH IN THIS section have shells similar to those found in crabs they differ in many other ways.

SHRIMPS AND PRAWNS

Shrimps and prawns of one kind or another are favorite baits with many salt-water anglers for a wide variety of fishes. In the south the smaller ones are called shrimp while the larger ones are known as prawns. Most shrimp are easily recognized since they look somewhat like small lobsters without the two, large claws. Instead, they have many tiny claws, a pair of long antennae and bodies which are often colorless, translucent or pale gray, green, blue or pink in color.

EDIBLE SHRIMP

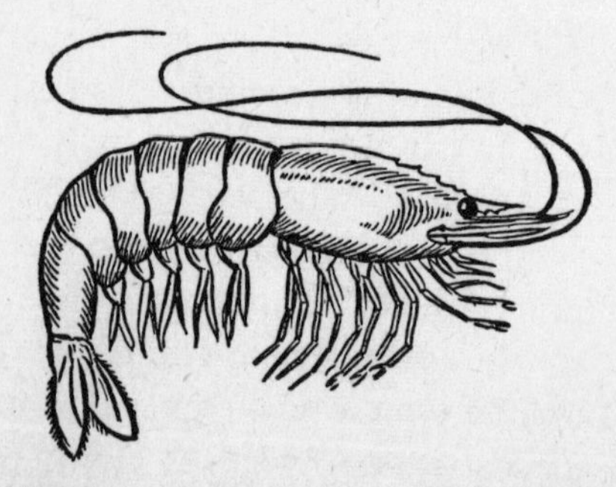

The edible shrimp (*Penaeus setiferus*) is the one which is usually caught by commercial fishermen and is found in the fish markets and restaurants. It is also called the common shrimp, southern shrimp, white shrimp, jumbo shrimp and prawn. This shrimp may reach up to 10 inches in length but most of those found do not exceed 6 or 7 inches. The edible shrimp is found from Virginia to the Gulf of Mexico. The adult specimens are usually found in deeper offshore waters, but the younger ones live in bays, sounds, rivers and other inside waters.

Two other shrimp related to the common shrimp above are caught by commercial fishermen. One is the Brazilian shrimp (*Penaeus brasiliensis*), which is found from Cape Cod to Florida. Another is the brown-spotted grooved shrimp (*Penaeus duorarum*), also called the "pink" shrimp, and is caught in large numbers in the Gulf of Mexico. Most of these large edible shrimp are caught by commercial fishermen either offshore in large boats or inshore and on coastal waters in smaller craft. They use mostly otter trawls, but cast nets and seines are sometimes used. The angler can often capture the smaller ones close to shore at night using minnow seines or dip nets. Shrimp are also sold by bait dealers, especially in southern waters where they are a popular bait. And of course, the tail sections of the edible shrimp are sold in most fish markets. The shrimp are sold alive by some bait dealers, but most of the shrimp are dead when bought and used. To keep them alive you need large tanks or bait cars where they have plenty of room and water. When dead they should be frozen or kept on ice. The tails can also be shucked and the meat can be kept in brine in jars for quite a while.

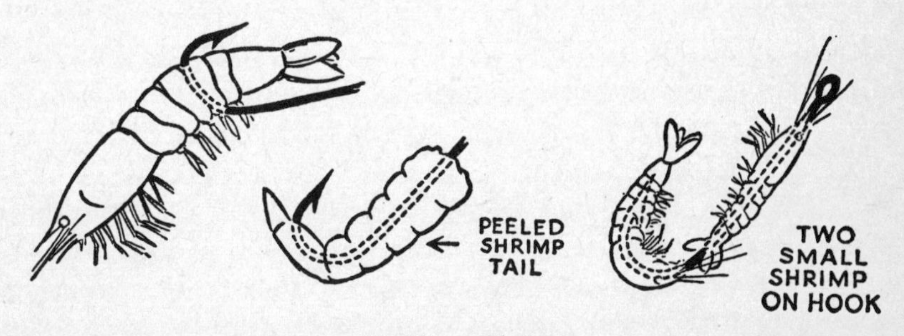

Hooking Shrimps

Shrimp are hooked in several ways, depending on the size of the bait, the fish sought and the method of fishing used. When using the live shrimp they can be hooked through the hard shell just behind the head. Care should be taken so that the vital parts are not pierced. These can be seen as a dark area inside the body. They can also be hooked through the tail at about the third or fourth segment. The smaller dead shrimp can be threaded on the hook running the point in at the head, then through the body and finally into the tail. With the larger shrimp, the tail section alone can be used, removing the shell and using only the meat on the hook. For small fish this tail portion can be cut into chunks of the desired size. When using just this meaty tail portion of the whole shrimp, the body and head can be broken up and thrown into the water as chum to attract fish to the area. Of course, in most of the edible shrimps this section is removed before the shrimp are sold on the market.

Shrimp are used for channel bass, striped bass, weakfish, bluefish, bonefish, grunt, pompano, snook, sheepshead, flounders, tarpon, snappers, grouper and many other fishes.

COMMON SAND SHRIMPS

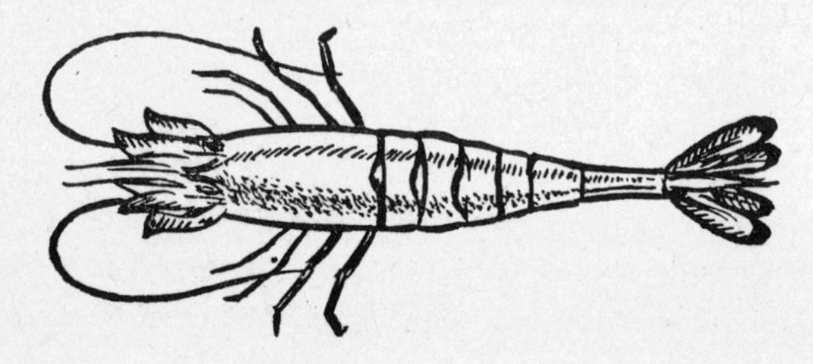

The sand shrimps which belong to the genus *Crago* include many species along both the Atlantic and Pacific Coasts. Although they rarely grow larger than 3 inches in length with the average closer to 2 inches, these shrimps are also used for food to a certain extent. They are commonly found in the shallow waters of bays, inlets, and sounds but also frequent deeper water offshore. They prefer sandy bottoms where they bury themselves but are also found hiding in the seaweed and among rocks. Sand shrimps are usually translucent, pale gray in color and flecked with spots of varying tints matching the bottom where they are found. They are sometimes called glass shrimp because of their clear glassy appearance. But this name is also applied to other small shrimps.

One of the most numerous sand shrimp along the Atlantic Coast is *Crago septemspinosus* or *Crangon vulgaris,* which is found from Labrador to North Carolina. It is also found along the Pacific Coast, but here the California shrimp (*Crago franciscorum*) is the one usually found. It ranges from Alaska to San Diego and is caught by commercial fishermen with trawls for the market. Another species, the black-tailed shrimp (*Crago nigricauda*) is caught in smaller numbers along the Pacific Coast.

But there are many other closely related forms found in Atlantic and Pacific waters.

The sand shrimps can sometimes be caught near shore in seines or dip-nets or in tidal pools along rocky coasts. They form an important food supply for fishes such as striped bass, weakfish, bluefish and flounders but can also be used for many other salt-water fishes.

COMMON PRAWN

The common prawn (*Palaemonetes vulgaris*), also called the grass shrimp, glass prawn, mud shrimp, harbor shrimp and pin shrimp, is a small variety reaching about an inch and a half in length. But it makes a good bait for many salt-water fishes. It is found from Massachusetts to the Gulf of Mexico in bays, ditches and estuaries over mud bottoms and in the eel grass. It can be distinguished from the sand shrimps by its longer antennae and the sharp spine it has between the eyes. It has a translucent, almost colorless body with brownish spots.

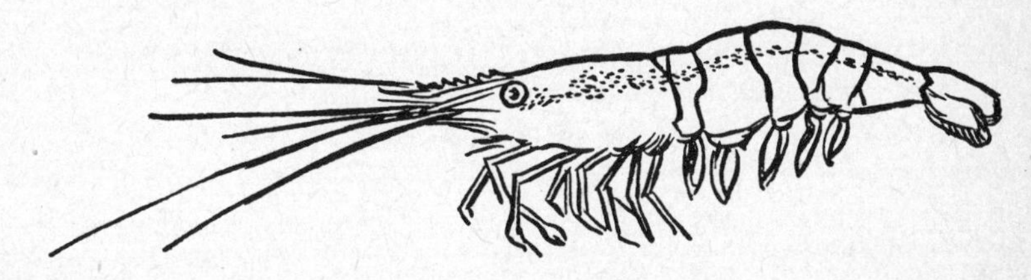

Common Prawn

Although the common prawn can be bought from some bait dealers and tackle stores, many anglers prefer to catch their own. Where they are fairly abundant this is often a simple job if you just need enough for one or two anglers. These small shrimp can be netted with a small dip net made of fine cloth or wire mesh. Look for them along the edge of the shore in coves, tidal creeks and flats. They are often found hiding in the eel grass.

For larger quantities a fine-meshed minnow seine can be used to obtain them. Of course, this is usually a two-man operation if a long net is used. One man can handle a small seine up to about 6 feet in length with the ends tied to poles, but beyond that length two men do a better job.

If you want to use the grass shrimp alive you can transfer them into a pail filled with sea water or put them in a bait car as you catch them. Although the small shrimp will live in a small container filled with salt or brackish water if it is changed frequently and kept cool, a large, wire-meshed, box-type container which can be placed in the water is better. This is best if you want to keep the shrimp for more than a day or two.

But if you want to keep shrimp alive just for the day's fishing you can pack them without water in almost any wooden box. One or more holes should be bored in the bottom and covered with wire screening. Then pack a layer of sawdust or wood shavings on the bottom of the box; after this add a layer of cracked ice. Now place a burlap bag over the ice. Then cover this with another layer of sawdust or wood shavings, after which scatter some shrimp over the stuff. Then add another layer of shavings or sawdust and on top place some more shrimp. This can be done with several alternate layers of shrimp and sawdust or shavings until all your shrimp have been packed. Finally on top of all the layers put another burlap bag soaked in sea water. Then place a cover on the box if you have one, but more important keep the shrimp box out of the sun and rain.

These small shrimp are very popular with anglers who fish for weakfish, since they make an excellent chum to attract fish to the boat. Just a dribble of one or two shrimp at a time thrown into the water will do the job if it is kept up without a break. But shrimp will also attract striped bass, bluefish, tautog or blackfish, porgies or scup and many other salt-water species.

To bait shrimp, they can be threaded on the hook head first and pushed up the shank until two or three cover the entire hook. This, of course, soon kills the shrimp and they'll live longer if you just hook them through the tail. One, two or three shrimp can be used on a single hook, depending on the size of the hook, and the preferences of the fish.

The common prawn will also take white perch, mackerel, flounders and many other fishes found in brackish and salt waters.

GHOST SHRIMPS

These shrimps are also known as burrowing shrimps since they live in underground burrows in mud flats or beaches. Three species are found along the Pacific Coast of which *Callianassa gigas* is the largest, reaching a length of 5 inches and is found from British Columbia to Lower California. Another common ghost shrimp is *Callianassa californiensis,* which is found from Alaska to Lower California. The two species above prefer the bays where there are mud flats. The third species, *Callianassa affinis,* prefers open beaches along rocky shores in Southern California. Another ghost shrimp is found along the Atlantic shore but it is not a well-known bait there.

The ghost shrimps are pink or cream-colored and have one large claw which either extends out ahead of the creature or is folded back over the front half of the body. These shrimp can be dug with a shovel or fork on the mud flats at low tide. Although they may burrow anywhere up to 3 feet, most of them do not go deeper than 20 inches or so. After turning over the mud or sand with the fork search through it quickly but thoroughly to find the shrimp. They can be used for halibut, croakers, white sea bass, sculpins and many other fishes found along the Pacific Coast.

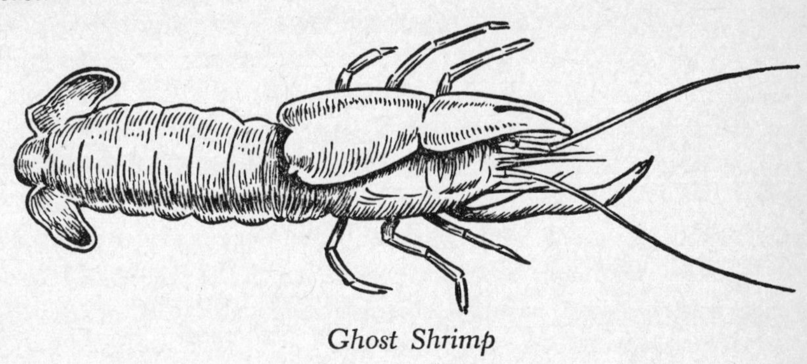

Ghost Shrimp

Of course, this list of shrimps and prawns is far from complete and there are many other varieties which are found along both the Pacific and Atlantic Coasts which can be used when they can be obtained in sufficient quantities.

SAND BUGS

The sand bug (*Emerita talpoida*) is also called the beach bug, sand crab, mole crab and mole shrimp. It is also known as the sand flea but this confuses it with the true sand fleas or beach fleas which are much smaller.

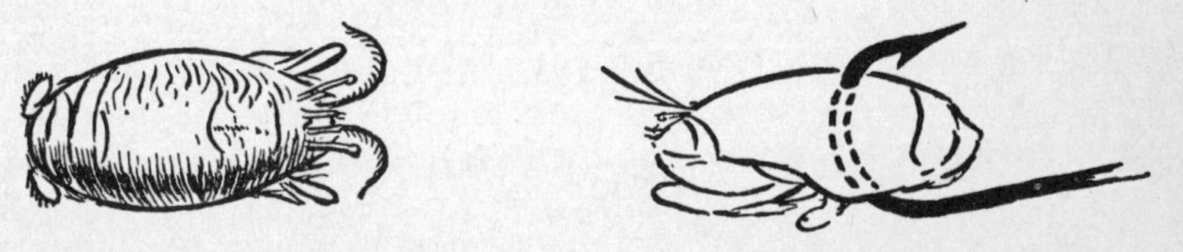

Sand Bug and Method of Hooking

The sand bug is easily recognized by the oval or egg-shaped body, smooth back and several stout, hairy legs on the underside. They may reach up to an inch and a half in length but usually average somewhat smaller. The shell is tan or sand-colored tinged with pink or light purple. The Atlantic species is found from Cape Cod to Florida, while a related form (*Emerita analoga*) is found along the Pacific Coast from Oregon to Panama.

The sand bugs are found along the open sand beaches where they burrow into the sand directly under the breaking surf. An incoming wave causes them to leave the sand and swim about, but as soon as the wave starts receding they burrow into the sand again. They move up the beach on an incoming tide and back again to low-water mark on the outgoing tide. However, sometimes they get stranded near high-water mark when the tide drops and can be found buried in the sand.

Sand bugs live in colonies numbering in the hundreds or thousands and they usually give themselves away by tell-tale streaks caused by the slightly protruding head parts as they burrow into the sand backward. Sometimes they can be found swimming around in tide pools, but usually they have to be dug from the wet sand under the breaking waves in order to obtain them. This can often be done by waiting until a wave sweeps up the beach and then, as the water recedes, digging your hands into the sand as deep as possible and feeling for the sand bugs as you pull against the rushing water.

However, the quickest way to obtain the sand bugs in large numbers is to make a scoop trap with a long handle. This can be made in a variety of forms, but usually resembles a giant dustpan with the long handle facing toward the opening instead of away from it as the conventional scoop. The frame can be made from wood or heavy wire and covered with quarter-inch or half-inch wire mesh. The larger mesh is better since it permits most of the sand and debris to escape. To catch the sand bugs all you have to do is wait until a wave sweeps up the beach, then drop your scoop into the receding wave and drag it toward you with the bottom of the trap scraping lightly against the sand. If you pick a spot where the sand bugs are numerous a few scoops will give you all the bait you need.

The sand bugs can be kept in damp sand in a container for quite a while. But since they are usually available during the fishing season a fresh supply can be obtained as needed. Most of the sand bugs you catch will be hard shelled ones, but a few may be soft shelled, especially during the summer months. These make very good bait but do not stay on the hook too well and may have to be tied down with thread. A single hard shelled sand bug can be hooked for smaller fish by running the point through the underside and out through the top shell. This should be done carefully so as not to make too large a hole or crack the shell. For larger fish several sand bugs can be threaded on the hook, shank and even the leader or snell. Sand bugs can be used for striped bass, channel bass, bonefish, sheepshead, tautog or blackfish, pompano, corbina, spotfin and yellowfin croakers and other salt-water fishes.

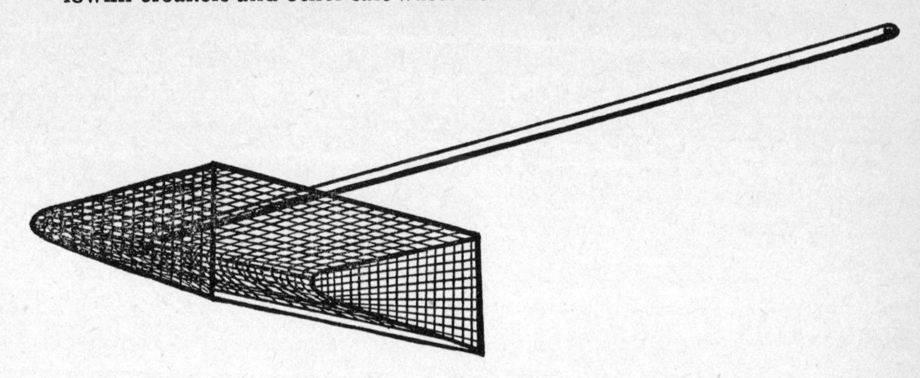

Scoop Trap for Catching Sand Bugs

SPINY LOBSTERS

The spiny lobsters which are found in tropical waters are easily recognized since they resemble the common lobster and fresh-water crayfish except that they lack the two large, pincer claws. In fact, they are often called salt-water crayfish. They are also called rock lobsters but this name is usually applied to those which are imported from South Africa for food. Spiny lobsters are blue, yellow and brown in color and are covered with many spines. The Atlantic spiny lobster (*Panulirus argus*) is found in Florida, the Bahamas and West Indies. A closely related species, *Panulirus interruptus,* is found in Pacific waters as far north as Southern California.

Spiny lobsters live in coral reefs, rocky bottoms and under kelp, hiding during the day and coming out at night to search for food. They are usually caught commercially in traps with funnel entrances which are baited with dead fish and are lowered to the bottom. They can also be speared by wading in shallow water or diving in deeper water and searching for them in their hiding places where they often give themselves away by revealing the two long antennae. They should be handled carefully to avoid the sharp spines on the back and antennae. Spiny lobsters are often sold in fish markets for food, but at prices which makes them an expensive bait. If you plan to catch your own spiny lobsters check the laws to find out the seasons, size limits and other regulations governing their capture in some areas.

The spiny lobsters can be kept alive in large crates suspended in salt water. The tail is the part usually used for bait and the hard shell covering is removed leaving the light meat. The head, body section and legs can be crushed and thrown into the water to attract fish. Spiny lobsters are favored for bonefish but can be used for snappers, groupers, grunts, sheepshead and many other fishes found in tropical waters.

COMMON LOBSTER

The common or American lobster (*Homarus americanus*) is known to practically everyone as a popular sea food. It also makes a good bait for many salt-water fishes but because it is so popular as food and expensive in price it is rarely used now. At one time back in the 1800's when lobsters sold for a penny a piece, lobster tails were used in striped bass fishing. They can still be used for striped bass, cod, blackfish or tautog and many other salt-water fishes. But unless they can be caught or obtained cheaply they are rarely used for this purpose today. Catching them in large numbers requires considerable equipment in the way of a boat, lobster pots, buoys and ropes. A few can sometimes be taken near shore in shallow water by wading or diving. Lobsters are found from Labrador to North Carolina along the Atlantic Coast, but are most numerous in New England and Canadian waters. Fewer lobsters are caught now than in the past, but the demand for them increases so they bring fancy prices on the market. To maintain the lobster fishery, the spawning females are protected, size limits have been established and artificial propagation is carried on at a few hatcheries. Thus it is doubtful whether lobsters will ever become so numerous again that they will be widely used for bait.

Chapter VII

BAITFISHES

THE BAITFISHES FOUND IN SALT WATER ARE NUMEROUS BOTH IN NUMBERS and species and are a favorite food with most gamefishes. They range in size from 2 or 3 inches to 2 feet or more with a weight of several pounds. They are found in the open ocean often many miles offshore as well as in the surf, bays, inlets, rivers and even fresh water. They are generally found in schools ranging from a few individuals to hundreds of thousands. These minnows of the sea seem to spend their entire lives battling the waves, currents and fleeing or hiding from birds and larger fishes.

CATCHING, KEEPING AND PRESERVING

Before we take up the individual baitfish themselves perhaps it would be best to discuss general methods of obtaining and keeping these baits. The most efficient and quickest method of obtaining baitfish in large numbers is usually by means of a seine. Small seines of 4, 5 or 6 feet in length can be handled by one person but longer ones require two or more men. In shallow water, seines can be hauled by wading but in deeper water one or two boats are needed. The general procedure is to start some distance away from shore and to draw the seine toward land, forming a half-circle so that the two ends of the seine touch land and cut off the escape of the baitfish. Another way is to anchor one end on shore and swing the other end around until it touches land, then pulling the seine toward shore.

The best time for seining is usually at low tide when the baitfish are concentrated in a smaller area. Another good time is at night when the baitfish hug the shore line in compact schools to escape the larger gamefish. But before you do any seining check your state laws to find out if there are any regulations on the subject. Some states require a permit or specify the length, mesh and width of the seine used.

Another way to obtain baitfish is by means of a "drop" or "umbrella" type net, which is usually square in shape and has lines attached to each corner for lifting. There are many types and designs on the market which can be bought cheaply. Or you can make one using wire, line and cheesecloth, mosquito netting or wire screening. They can be any size from 3 to 10 feet square. The smaller ones are best because they can be worked by hand. The larger ones require supports or pulleys. There are portable ones on the market which are small, and have a collapsible frame.

These drop nets can be lowered to the bottom in shallow water or to a depth of a few feet in deeper water where certain kinds of baitfish gather. Then soaked bread, crushed clams, crabs or shredded fish can be dropped above the net and allowed to sink into it. When the baitfish are thick over the net, it is quickly lifted to catch them. After a while the baitfish become suspicious and you'll have to wait longer or try a new area.

Still another way to catch baitfish is by means of traps. These can be bought in tackle stores and come in a variety of shapes, sizes and materials. They are usually designed for fresh-water minnows, but can be used in salt water for many kinds of baitfishes. They are round or rectangular and are made of wire, glass, plastics or cloth mesh. They have one or more funnel entrances through which the baitfish can enter, but find it hard to escape once inside. You can also make your own traps using wire screening or wire mesh molded around a wood or wire frame.

These baitfish traps are baited with bread, crushed clams, mussels or crabs, shredded meat or fish and similar foods. Then they are lowered to the bottom where baitfish are plentiful. In deep water it is a good idea to tie a buoy to the trap so that it can be located. In a swift tidal current or river it may be necessary to weigh down the trap with stones or similar weights so that it isn't carried away. The same thing can be done when there is a strong wind or storm, but the safest policy then is to remove the traps from the water.

If you want to catch plenty of bait with funnel traps you will generally need more than one or two traps. For best results these traps should be examined every few hours during the day and removed from the water before dark unless you also want to catch eels. Otherwise the eels will enter your traps during the night and eat up your baitfish.

You can also use a cast net to catch baitfish. This is a circular-shaped net which comes in various diameters and is thrown so that it spreads out like a parachute over the baitfish. There is a cord attached to the center which is tied to the wrist. The outer edge of the net is lined with weights which causes the net to sink like an inverted cup trapping the baitfish. It takes a while to acquire the skill needed to use a cast net, but it pays to own such a net and learn how to use it for those days when baitfish cannot be obtained by other means.

Some of the baitfishes can also be caught on hook and line using tiny hooks baited with bits of sea worm, clam or crab. A few can also be captured at times when they are in compact schools by kicking them out of the water with your feet or scooping them out with your hands. Or small numbers can be snagged with treble hooks or lures such as plugs. Baitfish are also washed out on the beach at times and can be picked up.

Of course, baitfish of various kinds are sold by tackle stores, boat liveries, commercial fishermen and bait dealers. But they do not always have baitfish on hand so many anglers prefer to catch their own.

After the baitfish are caught if you want to keep them alive transfer them immediately to a large container of salt water. Small numbers of baitfish can be kept in minnow buckets such as those used in fresh-water fishing. For longer periods of time the baitfish should be kept in bait cars or live boxes which can be nothing more than a wooden box with slits or screened sides and a cover and hinged door through which baitfish can be removed. Another type is a wooden frame which is covered with wire mesh on all sides forming a wire cage. However, only certain kinds of baitfish can stand prolonged confinement in a bait car. Many others are too delicate to stand the handling or confinement and soon die.

But most of the baitfishes can be used dead and these can be kept on ice, or frozen, or in brine. The brine solution should be strong and in an airtight jar for best results. Baitfish can also be preserved in a solution of one per cent formalin and 99 per cent water. The baitfish should then be packed into an airtight jar and the solution poured into it. If the solution starts discoloring it should be spilled out and fresh solution should be poured into the jar. This can be done two or three times or until the solution remains clear. If the baitfish are stiff you can use less formalin; if they are too soft add more formalin. From 5 to 10 per cent glycerin added to the solution will help to keep the baitfish soft. Baitfish preserved in such solutions are best when used in casting or trolling where they are used almost like artificial lures. For bottom fishing where the bait is still you can't beat fresh bait.

METHODS OF HOOKING

The basic methods of hooking baitfish are as follows: When still fishing with live baitfish run the hook through the back just in front or behind the dorsal fin, being careful not to strike the backbone. Another popular method of hooking is to run the hook through both lips from the bottom up. The baitfish can also be hooked through the side or belly. When using a dead baitfish you can thread it on a long-shanked hook by forcing the point into the mouth and out through the belly. Or you can run the hook through the eyes and then into the body near the tail. A variation of this is to run the hook through the mouth and out of one of the gill openings, then into the body.

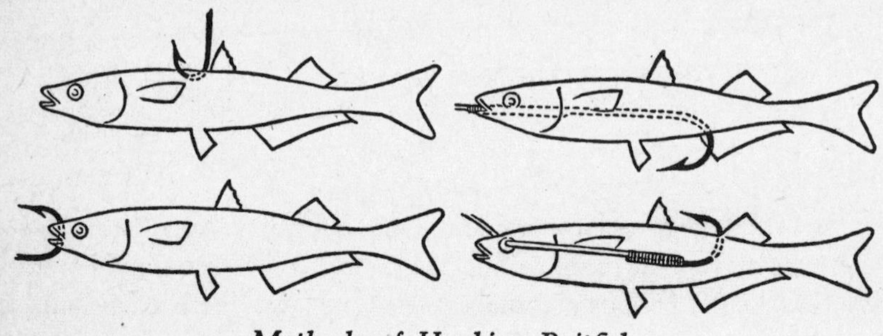

Methods of Hooking Baitfish

Baitfish can also be "sewed" on the hook so that they will have a permanent bend which will cause them to spin or wobble when pulled through the water. One of the simplest methods is to run your hook into the baitfish's mouth and out of the gill opening. Then tie a half-hitch around the baitfish's body just back of the head and insert the hook about midway between the dorsal fin and tail. Finally you tighten up on the leader, putting a bend into the minnow and secure the half-hitch.

But since baitfish vary in structure and there are many kinds of fishing in salt water, other methods of hooking are often used. Many of these will be described in the sections dealing with the individual fishes below.

MULLET

There are many species of mullets found throughout the world and they are especially numerous in tropical waters. And wherever found they are a favorite food of the larger salt water fishes and make good bait. Two species are commonly found in United States waters and these are the ones usually used for bait. The striped mullet (*Mugil cephalus*), also called the common mullet and jumping mullet, is one of the most abundant being found from Cape Cod to Brazil along the Atlantic Coast and from Southern California to Chile along the Pacific Coast. It has a dark blue back, silvery sides and noticeable dark stripes along the upper part of the body. The white mullet (*Mugil curema*), also known as the silver mullet, is likewise found from Cape Cod to Brazil, but it is more numerous along its northern range than the striped mullet. The white mullet looks much like the striped mullet except that its back is more olive-green in color and it lacks the dark stripes giving it a more silvery appearance. The striped mullet may reach 2 feet in length and the white mullet 3 feet, but most of those found usually run between 3 inches and a foot in length.

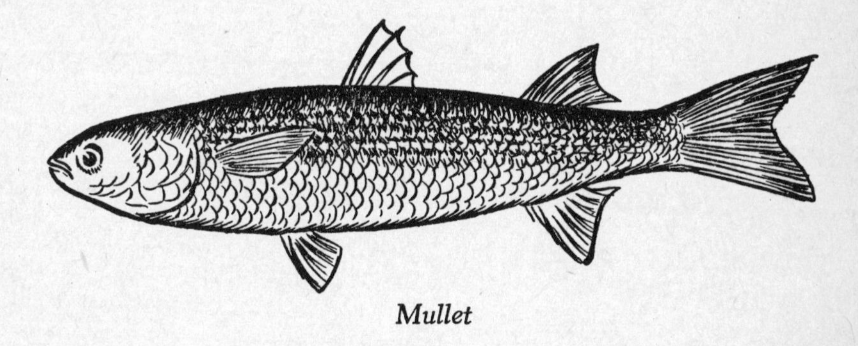

Mullet

Mullet are usually found in bays, sounds, inlets and rivers, where they feed on the bottom mud and sand, obtaining organic matter from these materials. They usually spend the summer months in these protected waters, then in the late summer and fall months leave the bays and migrate southward along the coast in large, compact schools. They hug the shore line closely, swimming through the heaviest surf at times and can easily be seen by the dark patches and ripples they create on the water. They also leap out of the water when frightened or when chased by larger fish.

When migrating in these compact schools they can be caught with seines or cast nets. During these migrations they seem to stop only at night to rest or to escape the larger fish and rarely can be caught on hook and line. But they have been known to take a small hook baited with doughball or bread bait in certain areas. Mullet can also be bought from commercial fishermen, fish markets and some bait dealers and tackle stores.

Mullet usually die quickly unless they can be kept in large tanks or pools with plenty of water. Most of them are used dead as soon as caught or are frozen or kept on ice for future use.

For still fishing with live mullet, hook them through one or two lips or through the back. Another method used for tarpon is to run a flexible wire leader with hook through the mullet's mouth with the aid of a needle and then out near the tail. The bend of the hook ends up at the mullet's mouth. A variation of this is to run the needle with leader into the mullet

One Method of Rigging Whole Mullet

just back of the gill opening to the other side of the backbone. Then the needle is run along the backbone and out near the tail on the opposite side of the mullet from where it entered. Finally the leader is drawn through the bait until the hook shank is buried in the body at the head end of the mullet. Of course, in these methods the mullet soon dies and is used dead.

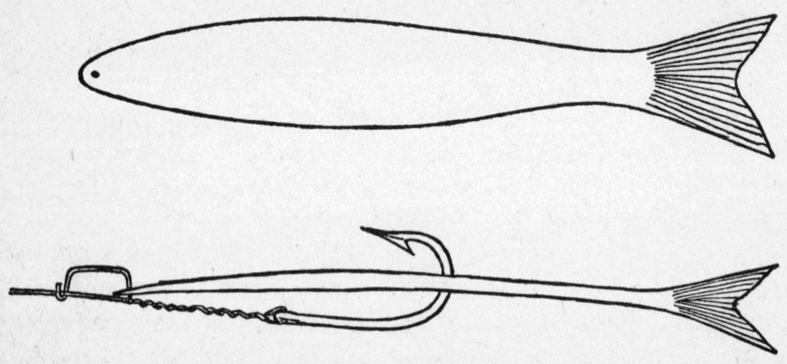

Split Mullet Bait and Method of Hooking

Mullet are also rigged whole in trolling for sailfish, tuna, marlin, dolphin, tarpon and other large gamefish. Here the backbone and intestines are usually removed and the hook is sewed in place so that it protrudes through the underside of the mullet and the leader emerges from the mouth. The mouth is sewed tight and lashed around the leader with cord. Other methods call for removing the head, dorsal fins and cutting the front part of the mullet at various angles, depending on the captain or guide who prepares the bait. Then the hook is sewed in place so that it protrudes through the underside of the mullet.

Mullet can also be scaled, the head removed and then split lengthwise along the backbone up to the very end of the tail. The backbone is taken out and the part near the head is then rounded off. This provides two split-mullet baits similar to the strip baits and is used on a safety-pin attachment with a single hook.

These silvery baitfish can also be cut into strips or chunks of varying sizes and used for bottom fishing. Most anglers scale the mullet before cutting it since the tough scales may lodge against the point of the hook and prevent penetration.

Besides the fish mentioned above mullet will also catch striped bass, bluefish, channel bass, weakfish, snook, summer flounder, grouper, snapper and many other salt-water fishes.

MENHADEN

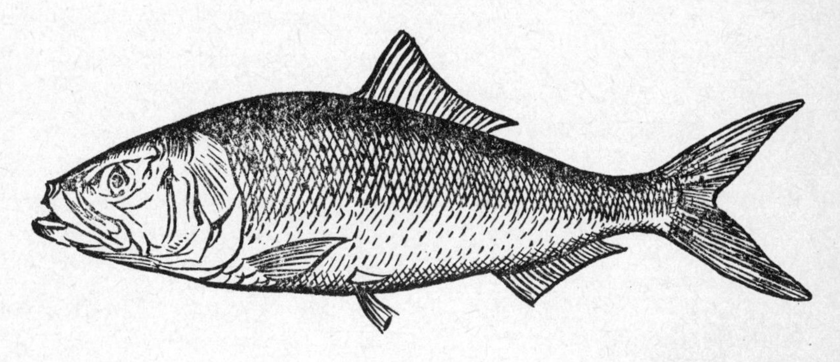

The menhaden is a member of the herring family and is a popular baitfish for many salt-water fishes. It has many names by which it is known in various areas, some of which are mossbunker, bunker, razor-belly, fatback, pogy or pogie, bugfish, hardhead, bony-fish, greentail and chebog. It is also called shad, shiner, herring and yellow-tail, but this confuses it with other fishes with the same names. There are several species of menhaden found in the Atlantic and Gulf of Mexico, but the most common is *Brevoortia tyrannus*, which is the one usually caught commercially and used for bait. It ranges from Nova Scotia to Brazil, and commercial fishermen catch huge quantities with purse seines to be processed into oil and animal and poultry feeds.

The menhaden is a flat, deep-bodied fish with a fairly broad back and a thin belly. It is colored bluish above with silvery sides which often have a brassy tinge. The adults have one large dark spot on the shoulder just back of the gill opening and smaller spots scattered along the upper sides.

It may reach 18 inches in length but most of those found run from about 4 to 12 inches in length.

Menhaden are usually found swimming in compact schools along the Atlantic Coast and in the bays, sounds, inlets and rivers. North of the Carolinas they are found migrating north in the spring of the year and south in the fall, while in more southerly waters they are usually present the year round. The schools of menhaden are usually easy to spot since they mill around in compact groups and create a characteristic ripple on the surface of the water. Or their bodies give the water a brassy tinge. Sometimes they will break water, especially when chased by larger fish.

Since menhaden are found in such compact schools and swim slowly or mill around in circles they can easily be caught by means of purse or haul seines. The average angler buys his menhaden from a commercial fisherman or bait dealer, but when they are found close to shore they can be caught in seines or other gear used in catching baitfish. Menhaden feed mostly on plankton—tiny plant and animal life—and are only caught on hook and line on rare occasions.

Menhaden are difficult to keep alive so most of those used are already dead and are preserved by freezing or icing. It is a very oily fish and will soften and spoil quickly. Freshly caught menhaden will stay on the hook fairly well, but when it softens it may have to be tied on with thread.

You can use large menhaden whole for the big gamefish like tuna, while the smaller ones a few inches long can be used for fish such as striped bass, channel bass or bluefish. They can also be scaled and filleted and the meat can be cut into strips or chunks. Or the menhaden can be cut crosswise into steaks of any thickness required. The heart of a menhaden is used for mackerel, while a hair net filled with ground menhaden and tied around a hook can be used for giant tuna.

Menhaden are also used in chumming for bluefish, mackerel, tuna and other salt-water fishes. A meat grinder is used to grind the oily menhaden and this is dribbled into the water to create a "slick" or chum streak which attracts the fish. This is a messy job and some bait dealers and commercial fish houses sell menhaden already ground up and frozen in blocks. Menhaden can also be cut up into chunks or used whole as chum for the large gamefish.

Menhaden can be used as bait for bluefish, weakfish, striped bass, channel bass, tuna, mackerel, sharks, rays and many other salt-water fishes.

ATLANTIC HERRING

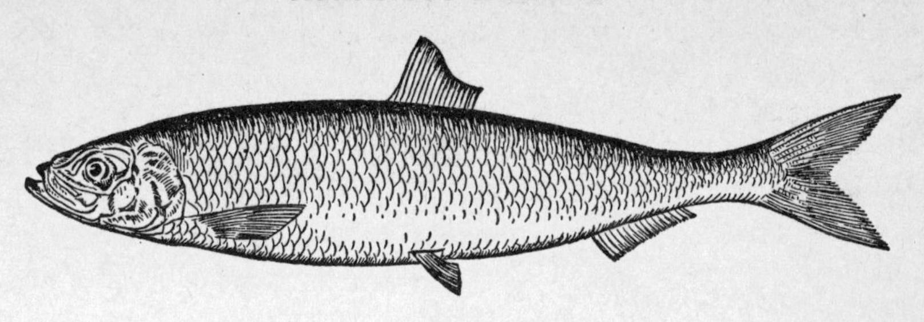

The Atlantic or common herring (*Clupea harengus*) is also called the sea herring and Labrador herring. Young herring are canned as "sardines" and are also called whitebait. The herring is one of the most numerous fish found in the North Atlantic with many millions or pounds taken annually and processed for food. The Atlantic herring is found from Labrador to Cape Hatteras, but is most plentiful north of Cape Cod.

Although the Atlantic herring is a thin fish like most of the members of the herring family it doesn't have as deep a body as the menhaden, shad or alewives. Its back is greenish or bluish and the sides are silvery. It grows up to 18 inches in length but most of the herrings found do not go over a foot.

The herring are found swimming in large schools and are taken commercially in weirs, seines, traps and dip nets. The larger herring can be taken at times on hook and line with tiny baitfish or small lures such as flies, spoons and spinners. They can also be snagged using lures or weighted treble hooks.

Herring are difficult to keep alive for any length of time unless you have very large tanks with fresh salt water circulating through them. They have a soft flesh and must be frozen or kept on ice at all times to prevent them from spoiling.

Likewise, herring are difficult to keep alive on a hook and soon expire, especially if they are caught and kept in a container for a while. The best way to use them alive is to catch them and then place them on the hook immediately when they are still lively. Although they can be hooked through the lips or back like other baitfishes, many anglers like to use tiny hooks and hook them along the belly. There are also rigs which can be made or bought to hold the bait securely without killing it too quickly.

When used dead for large gamefish, the herring is hooked through the back or through the lips in drifting or still fishing. For trolling the hook is sewn into the body cavity and is either buried entirely or allowed to protrude through the belly. Herring are also used in Nova Scotia as teasers for tuna. Here a dozen or so herring are tied about a foot apart and trolled behind the boat to attract the giant fish. They are also used as chum with whole herring or pieces of herring thrown overboard at regular intervals. They can also be ground up and used in the same manner as menhaden for chum. Strips or chunks of herring are good bait for bottom fishing.

The Atlantic herring when used for bait will take tuna, striped bass, bluefish, cod, weakfish, pollack and many other species.

PACIFIC HERRING

The Pacific herring (*Clupea pallasii*), also called the California herring, is the West Coast relative of the Atlantic herring. It is similar to the Atlantic herring in general appearance and reaches about the same size of 18 inches in length. The Pacific herring is found from San Diego north to Alaska in dense schools and is caught in large quantities commercially in nets and seines for food.

Like the Atlantic herring, the Pacific herring is fragile and difficult to keep alive. Most of them are dead when used for bait. The smaller ones are caught and used fresh while the larger ones are usually frozen. It can be hooked by many of the methods used for Atlantic herring and other baitfish. The herring is a popular bait for salmon in the Pacific Northwest where it is used in slow trolling. The smaller fresh herring from about 3 to 5 inches are rigged whole and are usually used behind a metal plate or spoon "dodger" which acts as an attractor. Here a needle is used to draw a leader through the vent of the herring and out the mouth. A treble hook is attached to the end of the leader at the vent and the shank is then drawn up into the bait's body. One of the hooks is buried in the bait, leaving two of them exposed. Some anglers also thrust a sliver of wood or a toothpick into the herring's eye; then bend the herring into an arc and force the pick in so that the bend stays in position. The mouth of the herring is also sewn or clipped so that it stays closed.

The herring are also "plug-cut" for salmon. Here the head is cut off at an angle slanting from the back to the belly and toward the tail. Then one or two hooks are used to hook the bait with the leader coming out at the front of the bait where the head was. The larger herring are used by cutting strips from their sides in the shape of pennants. The edges of these strips, or "spinners" as they are called, are then beveled on the inside meaty part and hooked with a single hook.

Besides salmon, the Pacific herring can be used for white sea bass, black sea bass, rock bass, halibut, Pacific yellowtail and many other fishes found in those waters.

PACIFIC SARDINE

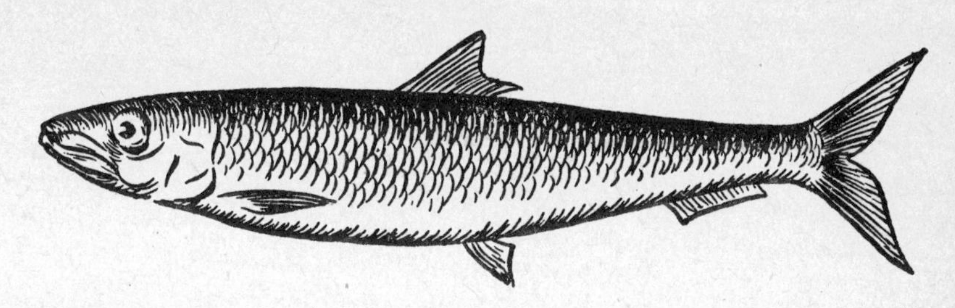

The Pacific sardine (*Sardinops caerulea*), also known as the California sardine, Monterey sardine and pilchard, is an important commercial fish on the West Coast; millions of pounds are taken each year for canning and for processing into meal and oil. Large numbers are also used by commercial fishermen and sportsmen as bait. The Pacific sardine is found from Alaska south to the Gulf of California. Since it also belongs to the herring family it resembles the Pacific herring somewhat except that the sardine has low, raised ridges on the gill cover which the herring lacks. And it doesn't quite reach the length of the Pacific herring, running only to about 14 inches. There are several other species of sardines found in U. S. waters.

Most of the sardines are caught by commercial or sport fishing boats in nets and seines. They are kept alive in large tanks filled with well-aerated water on the boats and are used for chumming and bait for many fishes such as yellowtail, albacore, tuna, bonito, barracuda, halibut and white sea bass. They are usually hooked through the nose or tail, but many of the methods used in hooking other baitfishes can also be used for sardines. Pacific sardines also make good bait for striped bass and the larger ones can be scaled and filleted or cut into chunks for this fish.

ALEWIFE

The true alewife (*Pomolobus pseudo-harengus*) is also known by many other names such as branch herring, river herring, wall-eyed herring, big-eyed herring, goggle-eye, spring herring, blear-eyed herring, buckie and Gaspereau. It is found from Canada to the Carolinas where it ascends rivers and streams to spawn. It reaches about a foot in length and resembles the shad in general appearance and structure. It is caught in large num-

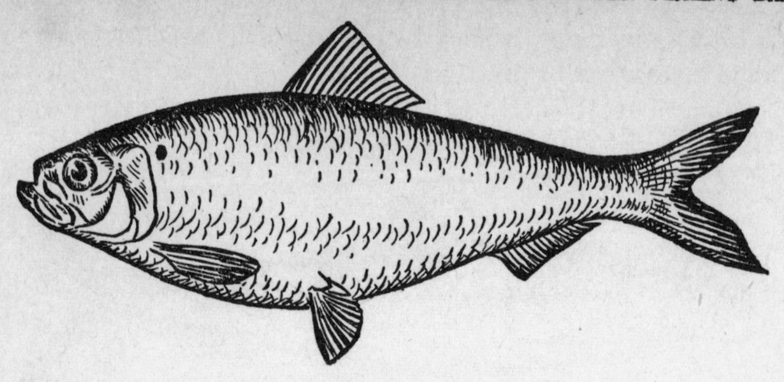

bers by commercial fishermen for food and can be used as bait for many of the fishes which feed on the other herrings.

GLUT HERRING

The glut herring (*Pomolobus aestivalis*), also known as the blueback, summer herring, May herring, school herring, blackbelly, sawbelly and kyach, is related to the alewife which it resembles closely. It is found

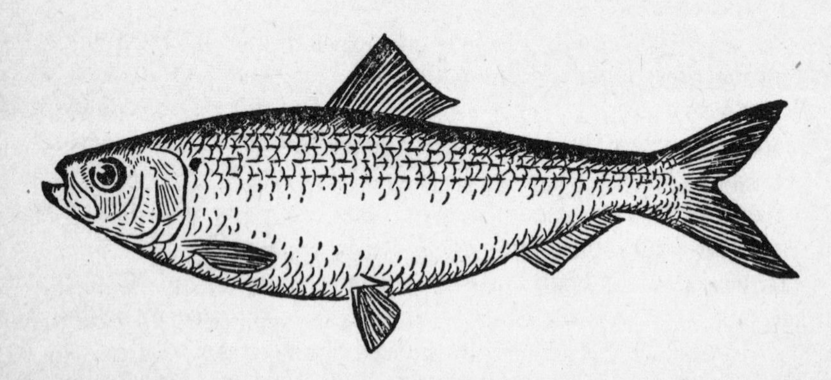

from Nova Scotia to Florida but is most numerous from Chesapeake Bay south. It also ascends streams to spawn but does not venture into fresh water like the alewife. It reaches about a foot in length and can be caught and used in much the same way as the other herrings for many of the same fishes.

HICKORY SHAD

The hickory shad (*Pomolobus mediocris*), also known as the shad herring, fall herring and tailor herring, is another species which resembles the alewife, glut herring and shad. However, it reaches a larger size than the alewife or glut herring, but not as large as the true shad. Some hickory shad reach 2 feet and almost 3 pounds. It also has a lower jaw which protrudes more than in the other herrings. It is a more active fish than the other herrings and feeds on larger foods, often chasing small baitfish.

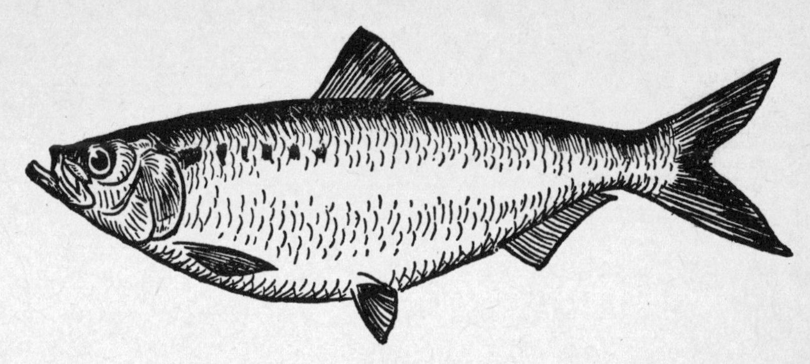

Therefore it can often be caught on hook and line and artificial lures. The smaller ones can be used whole, while the larger ones are cut up into sections or strips for many salt-water fishes.

ANCHOVIES

The anchovies are another large group of baitfishes which resemble the herrings somewhat in the compressed body shape and delicate flesh. Along the Pacific Coast two species are usually caught and used for bait. One is the northern anchovy (*Engraulis mordax*), also known as the California anchovy. It is found from British Columbia to Lower California and reaches about 7 inches in length. There are also two subspecies of this anchovy found in California waters. Another anchovy found in the Pacific is the deep-bodied anchovy (*Anchoa compressa*), also known as the sprat, which reaches about 6 inches and is found from Pt. Conception

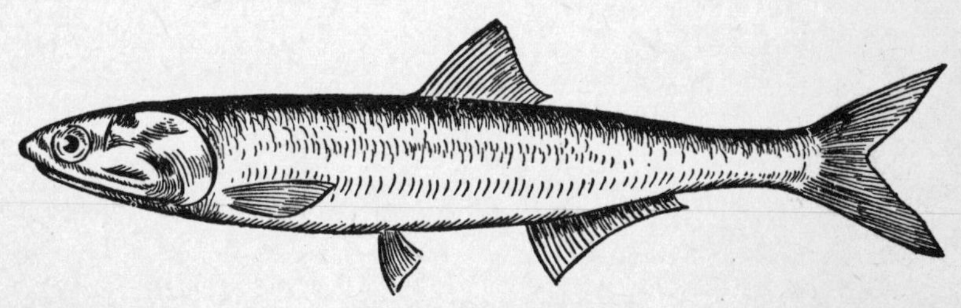

Northern Anchovy

south to Lower California. As its name implies it has a much deeper body than the northern anchovy.

The anchovies are widely used as bait in Pacific waters and several million pounds a year may be caught for this purpose. They are used for chumming and bait on commercial and sports fishing boats. And many of the methods used in hooking sardines and herrings can be used with anchovies. In Pacific waters anchovies are used for halibut, barracuda, yellowtail, albacore, sculpin, rockfish and many other fishes.

Along the Atlantic Coast the common anchovy (*Anchoa mitchilli*), which reaches about 4 inches and ranges from Maine to Texas, is quite numerous. Another abundant species is the striped anchovy (*Anchoa epsetus*), which reaches 6 inches and is found from Cape Cod to Brazil. Several other species of anchovies are also found in Atlantic waters. They can be used for striped bass, bluefish, weakfish and other fishes which feed on herrings.

There are many other herringlike fishes which can be used as bait when they can be obtained. Their delicate nature makes them difficult to keep alive or on the hook, but their soft, oily flesh attracts the larger gamefishes and they all make good bait.

KILLIFISHES

The killifishes of which there are many species are a favorite bait with salt-water anglers. The one usually used along the Atlantic Coast is the common killifish (*Fundulus heteroclitus*), also called the hardhead, mummichog, mummy, mud minnow and mud dabbler. It is found from Labrador to northern Florida, and another closely related form (*Fundulus grandis*) is found from Florida to Texas. They are easily recognized by the rugged body with single dorsal fin on the back near the rounded tail. In color they are a drab, olive-green with yellowish or whitish bellies. Some specimens have light, narrow vertical bars along the sides or small spots. They reach up to 5 or 6 inches in length. The killifishes are

Common Killifish

plentiful in most salt-water bays, tidal creeks and rivers right up to fresh water especially over mud bottoms where there are plenty of weeds. They are very gregarious and are usually found in large schools and can usually be caught in large numbers with seines, umbrella nets or in minnow traps baited with crushed clams, mussels, crabs or bread.

The killifishes are hardy baitfishes which will live out of the water and on the hook for a long time. They can be kept in damp seaweed for hours on a cool day. On hot days the container should be kept on ice or the killies should be kept in a minnow bucket or other container filled with salt or fresh-water. Unlike other salt-water baitfishes which cannot live in fresh water, the killies can stand the change and can be kept in fresh water almost indefinitely. But for best results if you want to keep them a long time put them in a large bait-box floated or submerged in salt water.

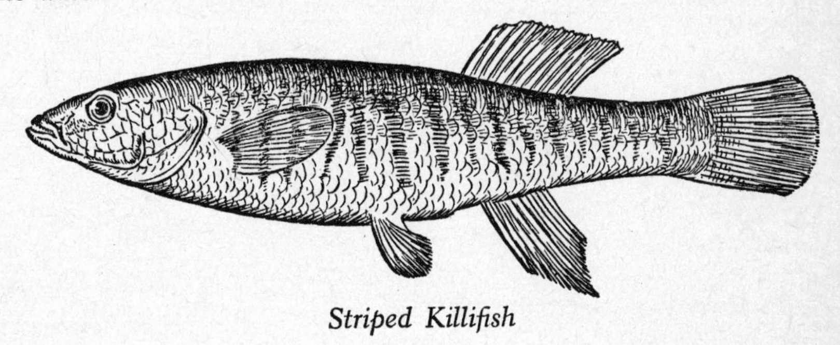

Striped Killifish

The killifishes can be used for many salt-water fishes such as striped bass, weakfish, bluefish and sea bass. They are especially popular for the summer flounder or fluke, and when these fish are running most of the bait dealers and boat liveries along the New England and in the New York-New Jersey areas carry the killies for bait.

Another killifish sometimes used for bait is the striped killifish (*Fundulus majalis*), also known as the Mayfish, bull minnow and bass killy. It is often found in the same waters as the common killifish, but it differs quite a bit in appearance and can easily be recognized. It is lighter in color, has a longer, more pointed snout, slimmer body and dark, vertical or longitudinal stripes along the sides. It also reaches a larger size with a maximum length of 8 inches. The dark stripes along its sides sometimes causes this baitfish to be mistaken for a young striped bass by anglers who catch them in their seines or traps. It is considered a poor baitfish by most anglers.

Still another killifish used for bait is the broad killifish (*Cyprinodon variegatus*), also called the sheepshead minnow. It is found from Cape Cod to Florida and has a much broader body than the common killifish. It rarely grows more than 3 inches in length.

SILVERSIDES

The silversides are often called salt-water minnows since they are very numerous in numbers and form an important food supply for many marine gamefishes. There are many species found along the Atlantic and Gulf Coasts but one of the most abundant is the common silversides

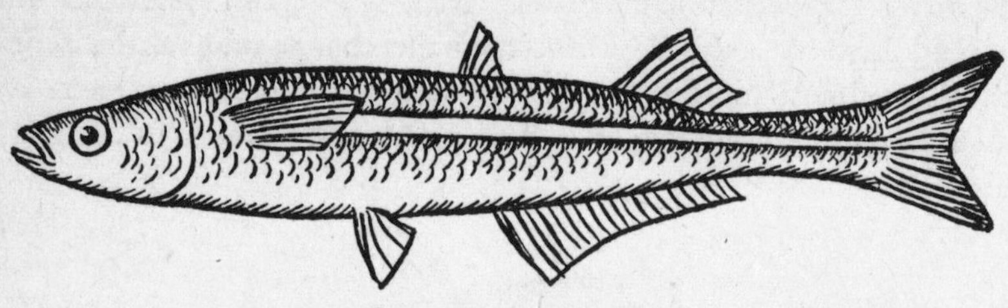

Common Silverside

(*Menidia menidia*), which is found from Maine to the Carolinas. It is also called the spearing, sperling, friar, sand smelt, white bait and shiner, but the last two names are also applied to other baitfishes. Along the Pacific Coast the grunion (*Leuresthes tenuis*), the jack smelt (*Atherinopsis californiensis*) and top smelt (*Atherinops affinis*) are not true smelts, but are also members of the silverside family.

The silversides are easily recognized by their pale green body color and the silvery bands running along both sides of their bodies. The common silversides may reach 5 or 6 inches in length but most of those found run from about 2 to 4 inches. They are present most of the year in some waters such as bays, rivers and surf, but are most numerous during the late summer, fall and early winter. They can easily be caught in seines, drop nets or minnow traps, especially at night. Silversides are also sold by many bait dealers and tackle stores. The larger ones sometimes appear in the fish markets since they make good eating. Silversides make good bait for many salt-water fishes, but they are rather delicate and die quickly in confinement or on the hook. But they are used dead for fish such as striped bass, weakfish, bluefish, mackerel, summer flounder or fluke, sea bass, cod and silver hake or whiting.

SMELTS

The smelts, of which there are many species along both the Atlantic and Pacific Coasts, often make a good bait for a wide variety of salt-water fishes. The American smelt (*Osmerus mordax*), also called ice fish and frost fish, is the most common variety along the Atlantic Coast and is found from the Gulf of St. Lawrence to Virginia. It lives mostly in tidal creeks, rivers and bays and goes up to fresh water to spawn. It is also found landlocked in fresh-water lakes. It reaches a foot in length but most of them range up to 7 or 8 inches. It is a popular food fish and is sold in fish markets. When numerous they can be caught with dip nets and will often bite on hook and line using bits of fish, sea worms and grass shrimp for bait. This smelt makes a good bait for cod and many other salt-water fishes.

Other members of the smelt family include the capelin (*Mallotus villosus*), found in Arctic waters and sometimes ranging as far south as Cape Cod, and used as bait for cod and other salt-water fishes found in northern waters. Then there is the candlefish or Eulachon (*Thaleichthys pacificus*) and the surf smelt (*Hypomesus pretiosus*), which are found along the Pacific Coast. Also the several members of the smelt family which are known as whitebait, which are found along the Pacific Coast. These Pacific smelts are used for many fishes such as salmon, white sea bass, barracuda, yellowtail, halibut and the bonitos and smaller tunas.

SAND LAUNCE

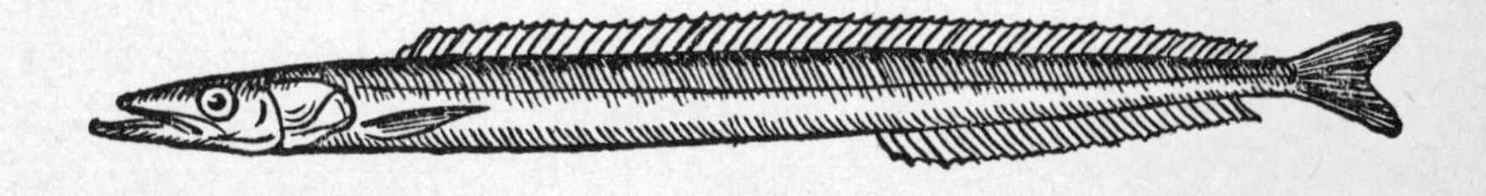

The sand launces, also known as sand eels, are an important item of food with many salt-water gamefish and therefore make good baitfish. They look like miniature eels and are found in huge numbers both in North Atlantic and North Pacific waters. But they usually reach less than a foot in length and they have a forked tail which the common eel lacks. Along the Atlantic Coast the common sand launce (*Ammodytes americanus*), which ranges from Labrador to Hatteras, is the species usually caught and used for bait and to a certain extent for food. Sand launces prefer sandy bottoms where they have the habit of burying themselves 5 or 6 inches in the sand. Along the surf they are sometimes left in the damp sand above low-water mark and can be dug up. Other times the sand launces can be found in large, compact schools swimming slowly and milling around over shallow and deep waters. Then they can best be taken in drop nets or seines. Sand launces are very abundant during the late fall, and during storms they are often washed up on the beaches high and dry or are chased there by larger fishes.

Sand launces are hardy baitfish and can usually be kept alive in damp seaweed for a few hours or so in cold weather. They are also a tough bait and stay on the hook well. A whole sand launce can be hooked through the eyes and then the hook can be imbedded in the body near the tail. The larger ones can be cut in half for smaller fishes. Sand launces can be used for striped bass, bluefish, weakfish, mackerel and summer flounder or fluke. They are also a popular bait for such fishes as cod, haddock and silver hake or whiting. Many salt-water anglers find them effective when trolled behind a spinner for fish such as striped bass, weakfish and bluefish.

This chapter includes most of the smaller baitfishes commonly used for bait in salt waters, but there are many others which the angler will come across that can also be used. Any small fish a few inches long can usually be used for bait with good results in salt-water fishing.

Chapter VIII

COMMON EEL

THE COMMON EEL (*Anguilla bostoniensis*), ALSO CALLED THE AMERICAN eel and fresh-water eel, is a favorite bait with many salt-water anglers for fish such as striped bass and bluefish. The common eel is found from Labrador to Brazil, and is most numerous in the bays, sounds, tidal creeks, rivers and fresh-water ponds and lakes. It is easily recognized by its snake-like shape. The eels vary greatly in body color, being gray, olive, brown or blackish along the back, and yellow, white or silvery along the belly. The females reach up to 4 feet in length but the males reach only about half that size.

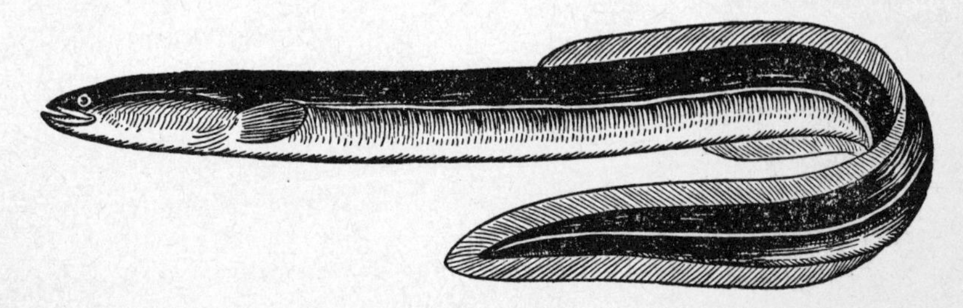

Common Eel

The common eel has an interesting life history which has been fully understood only since the early part of this century. It was found that they spawn in the ocean, southwest of Bermuda in the depths. After the young eels hatch it takes a year before they reach the coast and enter the rivers and bays. The female eels enter the rivers and head upstream spending their lives mostly in fresh water. The males remain in the salt water and brackish water of rivers and bays. The eels live there for several years until they mature and then in the autumn the females make their way down the rivers to the sea where they meet the males and they migrate to their spawning grounds to repeat the cycle.

Although both the female and male eels make good bait in salt waters, most of those usually taken for this purpose are the smaller salt and brackish-water males. They can be caught by many methods but the eel pot is the favorite and usually the most dependable. These are similar to the minnow traps with funnel entrances, although eel pots usually have wider openings to permit the larger, eating-size eels to enter. But for most bait purposes the regular wire-caged minnow traps or eel pots with small openings will work fine. These can be bought or constructed from wire mesh around a heavy metal or wood frame. Eel pots can be placed on the bottom of salt-water bays, tidal creeks and other bodies of water where the eels are known to be present. They should be set before dark and examined the following morning. They can be baited with meat, dead fish, crushed crabs, clams and mussels. Or you can place some bread in the trap and this will attract the smaller baitfishes which in turn will attract the eels. If the eel pots are set among the weeds or in deep or muddy water they should have a small buoy attached so that they can be found readily. The majority of the eels caught in the eel pots can be used for bait, but the real tiny ones can be turned loose, while the very large ones can be eaten or also released.

Eels can also be caught on hook and line, with small long-shanked hooks baited with pieces of fish, sea worms, shedder crabs or clams. However, this is usually a slow process and means fishing mostly at night, and the eels obtained are often too large. The eels are also taken by "bobbing," and here a dozen or so sandworms or bloodworms are strung on fine linen or silk thread and rolled into a ball. The whole mess is lowered to the bottom and when the eels bite into it they can be lifted out of the water and into a net or bushel basket.

When eels are numerous they can also be captured in seines. Or they can be speared at night by using a spear with several prongs and a strong light to pick them up on the bottom. Finally, eels can often be bought in fish markets or from tackle or bait dealers.

The common eels are very hardy creatures and will live out of the water for a long time in cool weather. They can be kept in damp seaweed if you plan to use them soon. For longer periods either tanks with running fresh water or wire cages suspended in salt water will enable you to have eels on hand whenever you need them.

Eels can be used alive for bait but they are so difficult to handle that most anglers use them dead. But a fresh, live eel is sometimes used for striped bass and here the best method of hooking is usually through the back or tail. They can also be hooked through the lips but often twist around the leader and line and make a mess of things. Eels can also be used dead or cut into sections for many salt-water fishes. They make a particularly good bait when crabs are around since fresh eels with the skin left on are tough and are not easily torn apart by the sharp-clawed bait stealers.

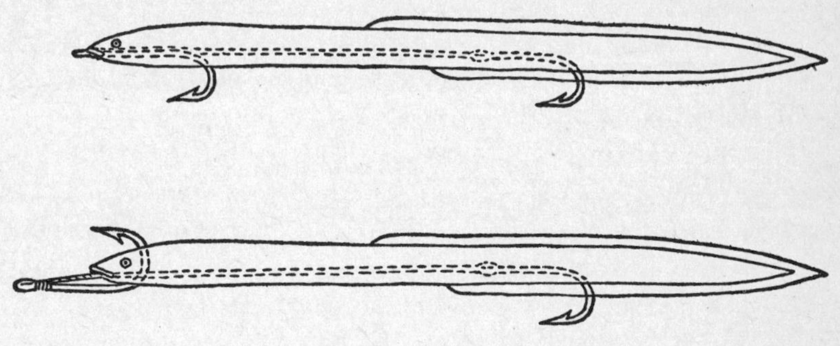

Two Methods of Rigging an Eel

One of the most popular ways of using the common eel is to rig it with one or two hooks and cast it out and retrieve it or troll it through the water to give it some action. Each angler has his own pet method of rigging a whole eel. Long needles are used to draw the line, wire, or light chain to which the hooks are attached through the body of the eel. When two hooks are used, the front hook usually emerges through the head or neck of the eel, while the other hook comes out near the vent a few inches from the tip of the tail. In most methods both hooks emerge on the underside of the eel, but in one method the hook comes out on top of the head. In still other methods small metal squids or metal plates are attached to the head of the eel to provide action and weight. Or the head is removed and the skin is pulled back and a lead weight is inserted to create an "eel-bob." The size of the whole eels used usually ranges from small 7 or 8 inchers to big 18 or 20 inchers, depending on the size of the fish they are used for.

The skin of the common eel is also used on various eelskin lures for casting and trolling. Most of these are usually a heavy metal tube, ring or weight with a hole to which the eelskin can be attached, permitting the water to inflate the skin when it is retrieved or trolled. Eelskins are also draped over a metal squid or attached to one by means of a ring.

Whole eels or eelskins which have been rigged can be kept for future use in large jars in heavy brine. The eelskins will keep for a long time in such salt preparations but the whole eels tend to get hard and then when they are removed and used they become soft. Although they will usually catch as many fish as a fresh eel, many anglers like to rig eels which have been recently killed because they do not tear apart so readily.

Eels and eelskin lures are used for such salt-water fish as striped bass, bluefish, weakfish, cobia and sharks, but other salt-water fish such as swordfish and marlin have also been known to take them at times. Preparing eels and eelskins is a messy job and more and more of these baits are being prepared commercially or by tackle dealers and can be bought in most coastal tackle stores.

Chapter IX

OTHER BAITFISHES

THIS SECTION WILL INCLUDE MOST OF THE LARGER BAITFISHES USED IN offshore fishing and those which were not dealt with in the previous chapter. Most of these baitfishes are used for such big-game fish as swordfish, the marlins, tunas and sailfish and they are often large in size. Catching and preparing these baits takes up a great deal of time, but it is a chore which cannot be avoided if you want to have a successful fishing trip.

PREPARING WHOLE, STRIP AND CUT BAITS

Most offshore anglers do not prepare their own baits since that is the job of the captain or mate on the boat that is chartered for this fishing. And since the art of rigging and preparing baits requires considerable practice, most anglers are content to depend on the fishing guides for their baits. Besides, each fishing area prefers different methods for preparing baits, depending on the prevailing conditions, and it is always best to follow the advice of the local fishing guides.

However, for the angler who must prepare his own baits a description of the methods commonly used may be helpful. A whole bait must be prepared so that it swims naturally and doesn't revolve when trolled through the water. In order to give the baits more action the backbone in the baitfish is often broken in several places or is removed entirely. The instrument for removing the backbone consists of a copper or brass tube with one end sharpened. This is pushed over the backbone, cutting it free from the rib bones. Then a wooden plunger is driven into the tubing to clean out the backbone left inside.

The simplest and quickest way to prepare a whole bait is to run the hook through the nose with the point facing either up or down. But this method has its drawbacks since it fails to hold the bait securely and is easily knocked off the hook by a fish or the resistance of the water. However, it can be reinforced by tying in the hook with line.

Three Methods of Rigging Whole Baitfish

One of the commonest methods of rigging is to insert the hook through the gills and then force it out through the belly. The hook is then sewn in place and in most cases the mouth and gill openings are also sewed up. In some baits a bridle is tied from the bait's mouth to the leader wire to keep it riding naturally. The hook can also be placed so that it comes out through the side or back of the bait.

A whole baitfish can also be slit open, the intestines and often the backbone removed and the hook is placed inside. The leader attached to the hook runs out through the mouth and then the belly and the gills and mouth are sewn up. Here the hook point can protrude from the belly or be buried entirely inside the stomach cavity.

Strip Bait on Safety Pin Catch Rig

Another method is to tie the hook ahead of the bait with a length of wire, chain or line as a connection between the mouth of the baitfish and the bend of the hook. Here the baitfish trails a couple of inches or so behind the hook.

There are many other methods used to rig whole baits and some of these are described in the sections dealing with the individual baitfishes themselves.

Strip baits cut from the sides and bellies of various fishes such as bonito, albacore, dolphin and mackerels are widely used in offshore trolling. They have various lengths, shapes and thicknesses, depending on the baitfish used, the fish sought, area fished or preference of the fishing guide or angler. Most of them run from about 8 to 14 inches in length and from an inch to 2 inches at the widest part. Both ends taper to more or less of a point with the front or middle of the strip usually being the widest part. The strips usually are from 1/8 to 1/2 an inch thick at the center and are thinned or beveled along the edges. Then the strip is impaled on a hook which is attached to a wire leader with a safety-pin catch which holds the front part of the strip. This front part of the strip can also be tied on to the leader with twine to hold it securely.

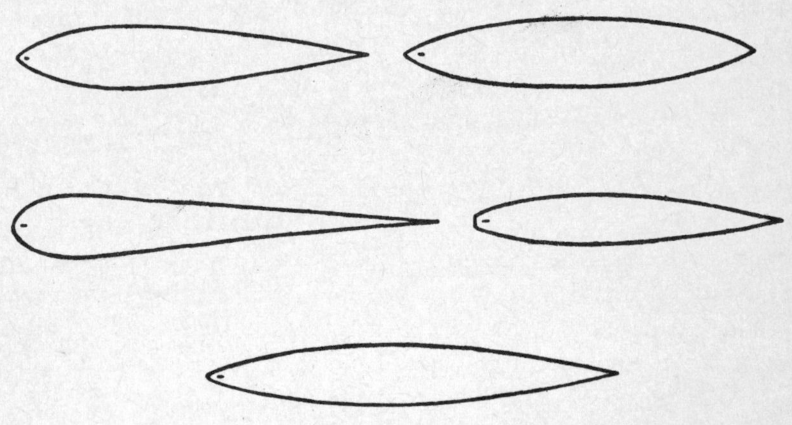

Some Shapes Used in Cutting Strip Baits

Other strip baits are made by cutting a portion from the belly of a baitfish, folding the strip and placing a hook between the folds. Then the strip is sewed along its whole length. A variation of this method is to cut two identical strips, place the hook between them and sew the edges, making a single bait. In both of these methods the fleshy part of the strips is hidden on the inside and the skin is on the outside.

Some of the larger baitfishes can also be filleted or cut into steaks or chunks and used as bait in still fishing. In most cases the baitfish should be scaled before being cut to the desired size.

Although frozen or iced baitfish can be used in an emergency to provide baits, they are not nearly as good as freshly caught baitfish prepared on the spot and used immediately for fishing. However, since fresh bait is not always available many anglers prepare their baits or strips in advance and keep them frozen or on ice until used. But freshly caught baitfish last the longest and usually make the most effective baits.

ATLANTIC MACKEREL

The Atlantic mackerel (*Scomber scombrus*), also called the common mackerel, is known to almost everyone as a popular food fish and to saltwater anglers as a fine gamefish and baitfish. It is easily recognized by its streamlined shape, blue or greenish color and the irregular dark bars along its back. It averages about a foot in length and a pound in weight but may reach almost 2 feet and weight of several pounds.

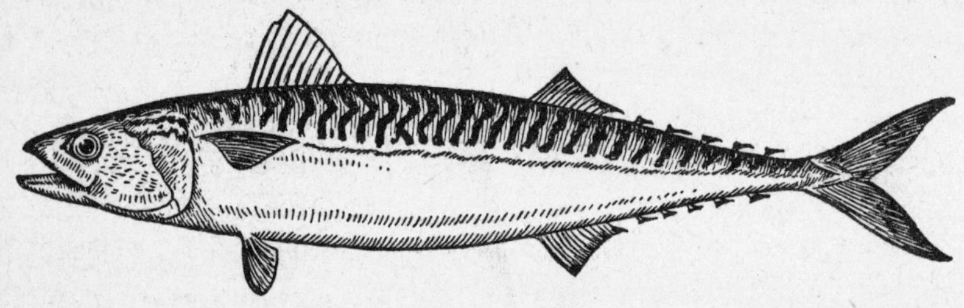

Atlantic Mackerel

Along the Atlantic Coast the mackerel ranges from Labrador to the Carolinas with seasonal migrations of vast schools of fish. They spend the winter in deeper, more southerly waters and the spring and summer in shallower, more northerly waters along their range. Generally the smaller mackerel are found closer to shore than the larger specimens.

The Atlantic mackerel are taken in huge numbers by commercial fishermen using purse seines and gill nets. Sports fishermen also catch many on rod and reel, for food, sport and bait. They can be chummed to a boat with ground menhaden and will strike pieces of fish bait or artificials such as spoons, flies, metal squids and jigs. And mackerel can also be bought in almost any fish market or from commercial fishermen when in season.

Mackerel can be kept alive for quite a while in large tanks or bait cars where there is plenty of fresh sea water circulating. They are used alive for fish such as tuna and can be hooked through the back. They are also rigged whole using either the regular method where the hook comes out from the belly or with the hook just ahead of the nose. The hook can also be placed inside the mackerel so that it comes out at the back near the dorsal fin with the point and barb facing toward the tail. These methods are used mostly to catch tuna and swordfish.

Tiny mackerel can be used whole and larger ones in chunks and strips for fish such as striped bass, bluefish, weakfish, summer flounder, pollack and cod.

Another species of mackerel, the chub mackerel (*Pneumatophorus colias*) is also found in the Atlantic from the Gulf of St. Lawrence to Virginia and resembles the Atlantic mackerel somewhat but it is not as numerous and rarely reaches more than 14 inches in length.

PACIFIC MACKEREL

The Pacific mackerel (*Pneumatophorus diego*), which resembles the Atlantic mackerel somewhat but is a closer relative to the chub mackerel, is an important food fish which is also used for bait. It ranges from Alaska to Lower California but is not common north of San Francisco. It reaches up to 2 feet in length and a weight of several pounds but most of them are under 18 inches in length.

Pacific mackerel are caught in purse seines, dip or scoop nets, gill nets, haul nets and on hook and line. They are caught by anglers on sea worms, clams, fish bait and artificial lures such as flies, spoons and metal squids.

They are used as bait alive for such fish as yellowtail and white sea bass and are rigged whole for swordfish. Pacific mackerel can also be cut into chunks and strips and used for many salt-water fishes found in those waters.

COMMON BONITO

The common bonito (*Sarda sarda*), also called the Atlantic bonito and northern bonito, is found from Maine to South America, mostly in offshore waters but occasionally it comes inshore to feed on smaller fishes. It is a streamlined fish with gray-blue back, silvery sides and dark stripes running obliquely along its back. It runs from about 3 to 10 pounds in weight with a maximum of about 15 pounds. It is fished for by anglers for sport or bait with artificial lures such as feathers, spoons, metal squids and plugs or natural baits such as strips or chunks cut from smaller baitfishes. There are also other species of bonitos related to the common bonito found in Atlantic and Pacific waters.

The common bonito furnishes strip baits for sailfish and the marlins. It can also be rigged whole for tuna, blue marlin and swordfish.

OCEANIC BONITO

The oceanic bonito (*Katsuwonus pelamis*), also called the oceanic skipjack, striped tuna and striped bonito, is found in the warmer seas but may range as far north as Cape Cod in the Atlantic and British Columbia in the Pacific. It is a heavier fish than the common bonito, with some specimens reaching up to 40 pounds, but is usually found under 20 pounds in weight. The oceanic bonito has a blue-green back, silvery belly and is distinguished by the lateral line which curves sharply downward below the second dorsal fin and four longitudinal stripes on the lower part of the sides.

The oceanic bonitos usually travel in large schools near the surface, chasing and feeding on smaller fishes. They can be taken on live baitfish such as sardines and anchovies or on artificial lures such as metal squids, spoons and feathers. The oceanic bonito provides strip baits and is rigged whole for swordfish. Large bonitos of 4 or 5 pounds are used in swordfishing and two methods are usually used to rig the baitfish. One used by Michael Lerner, the well-known big game fisherman, calls for removing the insides and backbone of the bait and sewing the hook either entirely inside the fish or protruding from the belly. The hook points face toward the head of the fish as in most rigged baits. The other method used by W. E. S. Tuker, who has taken many large swordfish off Chile, calls for cutting open the belly of the bonito and removing the insides, but leaving the backbone in the bait. The main difference, however, is that the two hooks are placed in the bait so that the points face toward the tail. The bait is then sewed up with the leader coming out at the tail where it is tied securely. Then the leader is brought back over the fish's back toward the head and is tied to the line which sewed up the bait's mouth. The bait is trolled head first, but when a swordfish strikes it, he cuts the line tying the fish's mouth to the leader and the bait turns around and faces tail first toward the angler.

SPANISH MACKEREL

The Spanish mackerel (*Scomberomorus maculatus*) is found along both the Atlantic and Pacific Coasts, being most numerous in the warmer waters. It is also called Sierra mackerel and spotted mackerel. It is a streamlined fish with deep blue back, silvery sides and belly and is covered along the back with bronze spots. The second dorsal fin which is yellowish and edged with black begins in front of the anal fin. The Spanish mackerel is usually found at the surface where it travels with others of its kind in large schools. It runs from 2 to 5 pounds in weight and may reach 25 pounds. It is a popular food fish, taken commercially in gill nets and purse seines. Sportsmen catch them on small metal squids, feather lures, spoons and flies. Two other mackerels closely related to the Spanish mackerel are the King mackerel (*Scomberomorus cavalla*) and the Cero mackerel (*Scomberomorus regalis*), which reach a larger size than the Spanish mackerel, but the smaller ones can be used for bait for many of the same fishes that take the Spanish mackerel. The whole mackerels and strips cut from the belly are used for the marlins, tunas and sailfish.

DOLPHIN

The dolphin (*Coryphaena hippurus*), also called the dorado, is easily recognized by its shape with the blunt head and long dorsal fin and gaudy coloring of blues, greens, purples and yellows. It is a fish of the open sea and is found both in the Atlantic and Pacific, and is most numerous in the warmer tropical waters. Along the Atlantic Coast it frequents the Gulf Stream and is often found hovering around floating boxes, logs, patches of weeds and other flotsam. Dolphin reach 60 pounds in weight but most of those taken fall under 25 pounds.

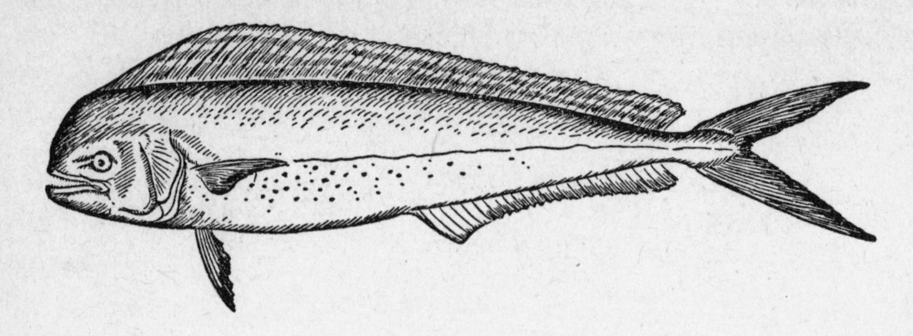

Dolphin are popular with anglers and provide a good scrap on light tackle. They will strike strip baits, feathers, spoons, metal squids and plugs. The smaller dolphin are rigged whole for fish such as the larger marlins, while strips cut from them are used for the smaller marlin and sailfish.

FLYING FISH

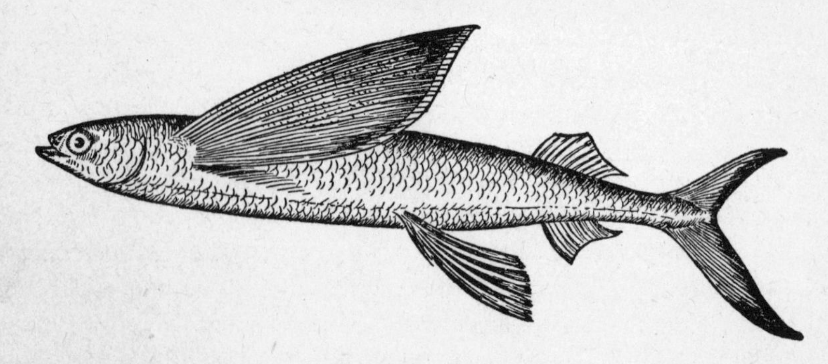

There are many species of flying fishes found in the warm waters of the world and most of them make good baits for the larger gamefishes. They are easily recognized by the long winglike pectoral fins, large pelvic fins and the extension of the lower half of the caudal fin or tail. Most of them are small and they range from 6 to 18 inches in length. Flying fish are usually found in the deeper offshore waters, where they travel in small schools under the surface and leave the water to glide through the air for distances up to several hundred feet when disturbed by a boat or larger fish. They make good eating and are caught for food or bait in gill nets or big dip nets.

Flying fish are used for tuna, sailfish, yellowtail, swordfish and the marlins. They can be hooked through the lips or by rigging the hook two or three inches ahead of the mouth which· is sewed up. Or they can be rigged with the hook protruding from the belly or side. The wings are usually tied so that they lie flat against the body.

NEEDLEFISH

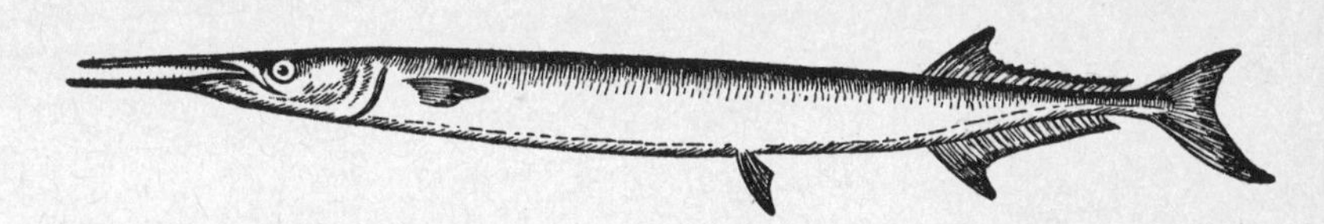

The long, slim needlefishes which belong to the family *Belonidae* are numerous in species and numbers in the warmer waters of the Atlantic and Pacific. They resemble the fresh-water garfish, being elongated and having long, thin jaws armed with numerous pointed teeth. They run from several inches to 4 feet in length and are known by various names such as garfish, needlegar, billfish, houndfish, agujon, sea pike, longjaws and timucu, depending on the species and locality where found.

Needlefish can be caught in cast nets or dip nets or speared at night. They leap out of the water or skim along the surface with great speed and can pierce a man's body with their sharp beaks. Needlefish can be used alive on a hook for many salt-water fishes and are popular for sailfish when rigged whole with the hook protruding from the back or belly.

HALF-BEAKS OR BALAOS

The balaos or half-beaks, also known as ballyhoo, resemble the needlefishes somewhat except that instead of two long jaws only the lower jaw

Half-Beak

is long in the half-beaks. There are many species found in warmer waters of the Atlantic and most of them run from a few inches to about a foot and a half in length. They can be caught at night by using a light to attract them and scooping them up with dip nets.

The half-beaks, which can be used for tarpon, amberjack, barracuda and sailfish, are hooked through the head or rigged so that the hook enters on one side near the tail and comes out through the other side. It is a soft baitfish and doesn't last very long on the hook.

MISCELLANEOUS BAITFISHES

There are many other baitfishes which can be used in salt-water fishing. One of these is the bonefish, which is a popular gamefish in tropical waters. It makes a good bait for the larger marlins and tunas.

The smaller albacores can be used whole for fish such as swordfish and marlin, cut up into strips for sailfish and marlin, or into chunks for sharks and other fishes. Strips cut from the various kinds of tunas can also be used for trolling baits.

The smaller barracudas can be used whole for sailfish, tuna and the marlins. Strips cut from the barracuda are also used.

Live blue runners are often used in drift fishing for sailfish or for amberjack. Likewise live grunts make good bait for barracuda, tarpon, Jewfish and amberjack. And the pinfish can be used alive for tarpon and amberjack. Other porgies can also be used alive or cut for various fishes.

The butterfish is sometimes used whole for tuna and cut up into strips for bluefish, weakfish and other salt-water fishes.

The silver hake or whiting makes a good bait for tuna. Ling and small cod will also take the tuna.

Small catfish hooked through both lips make a good bait for tarpon and are also used for Jewfish.

Strips cut from the whip ray have been used trolling for sailfish, and chunks cut from the various members of the ray family make fine bait for sharks.

Finally, in an emergency, pieces cut from almost any fish you are catching can be tried for the same kind of fish. Most fish are cannibalistic and strips of silver hake will catch other silver hake, strips or chunks of channel bass will catch other channel bass, strips cut from fluke or summer flounder will take other fluke, etc.

Chapter X

THE BAIT BUSINESS

MANY OF THE NATURAL BAITS USED IN FRESH-WATER FISHING CAN BE PROPAgated and the bait dealers can often raise unlimited quantities to meet the demand for these baits. But it is difficult or impractical to propagate the salt-water baits because they usually require natural conditions which are hard to create artificially. So almost all the natural salt-water baits are obtained from the ocean and other tidal waters as needed. The best that can be done is to keep the baits alive or preserved until they are used by the anglers.

Since salt-water fishing is seasonal in most areas, very few people devote all their time to obtaining or selling natural baits. The demand for salt-water baits in most areas runs from April to October and the peak months are June, July and August. Of course, the farther south you go the longer the season, and Florida, for example, is fished by many thousands of anglers during the winter months. But at best, the salt-water bait business is rarely an all-year-round affair.

Most of the salt-water baits are obtained, handled and sold by commercial fishermen, fish markets, boat liveries and tackle stores. The handling of natural baits is usually a side line with these places and their major incomes come from other products or services. The commercial fishermen, for example, obtain menhaden, herring, mullet, mackerel, squid, crabs and clams and other baits mostly for food or for processing into various products but often sell small quantities to sport fishing boats, bait dealers and tackle stores to be used for bait. If the demand for bait is large and the baits wanted are plentiful, some of the commercial fishermen may spend quite a bit of time trying to obtain them, but usually they stick to their main business of fishing for the food markets.

When it comes to sea worms, there is a fairly large business built around these baits along the Atlantic Coast from Long Island, New York, to Maine. The great majority of the bloodworms and clam worms come from Maine. The industry supports several hundred diggers, shippers and wholesalers who supply the retail outlets. To be a digger doesn't require much of an investment—a fork or hoe, a pair of boots, a bucket for the worms and he is in business. A digger can spend from two to four hours on the flats a day when the tide is low. During favorable seasons he can dig anywhere from 300 to 1000 or more worms a day, but as more and more worms are removed each year, the pickings become slimmer and fewer worms are taken. And the weather can affect the digging, since too much rain drives the worms deeper into the ground and hot weather kills the worms quickly. Digging worms is also hard work and seasonal. In addition Maine requires that a digger be a resident of the state for at least five years and take out a license. Small quantities of sea worms are also dug in Massachusetts, Rhode Island, Connecticut and Long Island, New York.

The digger takes his worms to the shipper, who buys them from him and sorts, packs and ships the worms to the wholesalers. The shipper must have storage space such as a cool basement where the worms are kept until shipped. He also needs large wooden trays and plenty of rockweed to keep the worms in.

The shipper sends his worms to the wholesaler, who is usually found in the larger cities and supplies the retail outlets such as the tackle stores and boat liveries. The wholesaler usually handles other kinds of baits besides worms.

Naturally, the opportunities in the well-established sea-worm industry are somewhat limited and those who want to get into the bait business will find less competition and more openings in handling other baits. The baitfishes such as mullet, spearing, herring and killies can often be seined in large numbers and sold to bait dealers or the anglers themselves. Some bait dealers such as tackle stores and boat liveries seine the baitfish themselves, but others are too busy and will often buy from anyone who can supply them with such baits. The equipment for seining baitfish is not too expensive and requires seines, a small boat or two when the fish are in deep water and two or three men to handle the operations. Of course, some baitfish such as killifish must be kept alive, and tanks or bait cars are needed to hold them. Others which die quickly can be frozen or kept on ice until needed.

There is also a very good demand for shedder crabs such as the blue crab and calico or lady crab. But these crabs are never obtained in very great quantities and it often takes a great deal of time and hard work to get them. The green crabs and fiddler crabs are often numerous and since they are hardy and live a long time out of the water, it is often profitable to handle them if they can be caught in large numbers.

The edible shrimps can be obtained from commercial houses and sold as bait to bait dealers or the anglers themselves. Other kinds of shrimp which are used alive must be seined in shallow waters and kept alive in tanks or bait cars or packed in various materials and ice until used.

During the height of the fishing season there is often a great demand for certain kinds of bait and if you can supply the retail outlets with the baits they need you can often do a good business. Many of these outlets run short of bait or have difficulty in obtaining them through regular channels and they will welcome a supplier they can depend on. Usually it pays to specialize in obtaining one or two kinds of baits since it takes plenty of time and work to obtain and handle several kinds of baits. Of course, if you act only as a distributor or wholesaler, you can handle a large variety of baits, but you must be situated in a spot where there are many retail outlets.

Many tackle stores and boat liveries sell natural baits to their angler customers, and although handling such baits is often a nuisance or not very profitable, these businesses realize that it attracts more customers. Many anglers like to buy their baits on or near the fishing spots and they will go to the tackle store or boat station which handles these baits rather than to a place which doesn't handle baits.

So at best the salt-water bait business is a part-time or seasonal venture, and because very few salt-water baits can be raised artificially it is limited in scope and can never hope to equal the fresh-water bait business. The fact that there are fewer salt-water anglers than fresh-water anglers also helps to keep the salt-water bait business smaller. But salt-water anglers are increasing in numbers each year, and in many areas and during certain seasons the demand for salt-water baits often exceeds the supply. If the bait dealers can meet this demand the resulting turnover makes it a profitable venture during the fishing season.

BIBLIOGRAPHY

Below are listed some publications which contain information on natural baits and which the reader may want to consult.

Angler's Handbook. Ted Trueblood. Thomas Y. Crowell Co., New York, 1949.

Bait Casting. Gilmer G. Robinson. A. S. Barnes and Co., New York, 1941.

Basic Fishing from Worm to Fly. Harlan Major. Funk and Wagnalls Co., New York, 1947.

Between Pacific Tides. Edward F. Ricketts and Jack Calvin. Stanford University Press, Stanford, California, 1948.

Common Marine Fishes of California. Fish Bulletin No. 68. Phil M. Roedel. California Division of Fish and Game, 1948.

Field Book of Insects. F. E. Lutz. G. P. Putnam's Sons, New York, 1935.

Field Book of Ponds and Streams. Ann Haven Morgan. G. P. Putnam's Sons, New York, 1930.

Field Book of Seashore Life. Roy Waldo Miner. G. P. Putnam's Sons, New York, 1950.

Fishes of the Great Lakes Region. Carl L. Hubbs and Karl F. Lagler. Cranbrook Institute of Science, Bloomfield Hills, Michigan, 1947.

Fishing the Atlantic. S. Kip Farrington, Jr. Coward-McCann, Inc., New York, 1949.

Handbook of Salt Water Fishing. O. H. P. Rodman. J. B. Lippincott Co., Philadelphia, 1952.

Insect Book. Leland O. Howard. Doubleday, Page & Co., New York, 1901.

Lee Wulff's Handbook of Freshwater Fishing. Lee Wulff, J. B. Lippincott Co., Philadelphia, 1944.

Life of Inland Waters. Needham and Lloyd. Comstock Publishing Co., Inc., Ithaca, New York, 1937.

Light-Tackle Fishing. Byron W. Dalrymple. Whittlesey House, New York, 1947.

North American Game Fishes. Francesca LaMonte. Doubleday, Doran and Co., New York, 1945.

Northern Fishes. Samuel Eddy and Thaddeus Surber. University of Minnesota Press, Minneapolis, Minnesota, 1943.

Pacific Game Fishing. S. Kip Farrington, Jr. Coward-McCann, Inc., New York, 1942.

Propagation of Minnows and Other Bait Species. J. R. Dobie, O. L. Meehean, and G. N. Washburn. Superintendent of Documents, Washington 25, D.C., 1948.

Salt Water Fishing. Robert A. Dahne. Henry Holt and Co., New York, 1950.

Salt Water Fishing. Van Campen Heilner. Alfred A. Knopf, Inc., New York, 1937.

Salt Water Sportsman's Handbook. Henry Lyman. Salt Water Sportsman, Boston, 1947.

Surf Fishing. Vlad Evanoff. A. S. Barnes and Co., New York, 1948.

Tackle Tinkering. H. G. Tapply. A S. Barnes and Co., New York, 1946.

Wise Fishermen's Encyclopedia. Edited by A. J. McClane. William H. Wise and Co., Inc., New York, 1951.

With Fly, Plug and Bait. Bergman. William Morrow and Co., New York, 1947.

INDEX